"Theologians have often noted that contemporary views of hell owe more to works like Dante's *Divine Comedy* than to the Christian Scriptures. Similarly, those who turn to the Bible for its instruction on hell are typically surprised by how little it actually says. For both reasons, this book by Paul Marston is a useful and welcome primer."

—JOEL B. GREEN
Senior professor of New Testament interpretation,
Fuller Theological Seminary

"In *Hellfire and Destruction*, Paul Marston offers a helpful primer on the case for conditional immortality or annihilationism, which is accepted by increasing numbers of evangelical Christians—not because of philosophy or sentimentality, but because the Bible teaches it clearly, as Marston demonstrates."

—CHRISTOPHER M. DATE
Editor of *Rethinking Hell*

"Paul Marston's book *Hellfire and Destruction* offers a well-researched analysis on the outcome of the final judgment. It thoroughly debunks the popular teaching of everlasting torment taught in many churches today and instead upholds the biblical view that the 'wages of sin is death' (Rom 6:23). The book is easy to read but thorough and an excellent contribution to the growing list of studies that reject everlasting torment. Highly recommended."

—KIM PAPAIOANNOU
Author of *The Geography of Hell in the Teaching of Jesus*

"By carefully reviewing the language, imagery, and argument of Scripture, Paul Marston offers a highly focused clarification that hell does not mean everlasting torment but final destruction. In so doing he helps those of us who identify as evangelicals to articulate the gospel as a testimony to the Judge of all the earth who always does what is right."

—NIGEL G. WRIGHT
Principal emeritus, Spurgeon's College

Hellfire and Destruction

Hellfire and Destruction

What Does the Bible Really Say about Hell?

PAUL MARSTON

Forewords by
DAVID WILKINSON
and ERNEST C. LUCAS

WIPF & STOCK · Eugene, Oregon

HELLFIRE AND DESTRUCTION
What Does the Bible Really Say about Hell?

Wipf & Stock
An Imprint of Wipf and Stock Publishers
199 W. 8th Ave., Suite 3
Eugene, OR 97401

www.wipfandstock.com

PAPERBACK ISBN: 978-1-6667-8478-7
HARDCOVER ISBN: 978-1-6667-8479-4
EBOOK ISBN: 978-1-6667-8480-0

VERSION NUMBER 120723

Contents

Permissions

Scripture quotations in this publication are generally taken either from the ESV or the NRSV as noted:

Some verses may be taken from the:

WEB (Word English Bible) Public Domain Version

NET (New English Translation)

LXX stands for Septuagint, the third- to second-century BCE translation of the Old Testament into Greek that was in common use by Jews in the first century.

Any italics in quotations of Scripture have been added by the author.

Foreword

by David Wilkinson

Why is it that occasionally the beliefs of those who believe in the Bible are far more influenced by culture, tradition and philosophy rather than the Bible? Sometimes beliefs seen by many as orthodox to the evangelical tradition are not rooted in the careful and complex task of interpreting scripture with attention given to its original context and authorial intention. This does not happen often but when it does happen, the role of the evangelical theologian is to unpack this and point back to the Bible.

This is what Paul Marston does in this fascinating and important book, *Hellfire and Destruction*. While evangelicals have been clear and united about doctrines of salvation and judgment, they have differed and fallen out over the consequences of judgment for those who ultimately reject the grace of salvation. This book goes back to the Bible, carefully engaging with biblical texts, words, and themes to deliver powerful arguments against a picture of a vindictive God sustaining hell as a place of eternal torment.

Paul Marston is thoroughly committed to the authority of scripture and it is because of this that he wants to be clear about what scripture says and what it does not say to a question which has been struggled with by academic theologians, preachers, and those who have lost loved ones. All of these groups will find not just something of worth in this book but authenticity to sustain mission, ministry, and discipleship.

Rev'd Professor David Wilkinson

Principal of St John's College, Durham

Foreword
by Ernest C. Lucas

The argument of this book, that hell in the New Testament does not refer to unending torment but to an ultimate fate of nonexistence following final judgment and period of punishment, is not new. It is found in the teaching of early Christian scholars, for example Justin Martyr and Irenaeus, and has continued to have supporters since. It is good to have a fresh statement of it in a book which deals with it in some depth while not being too lengthy. Marston presents his argument clearly and well, dialoguing with scholars who hold other views. He both responds to their critique of the position he holds and exposes weaknesses in their positions. All the key biblical passages that are relevant to the debate are discussed in some detail. He puts forward a strong and coherent argument that deserves serious consideration.

Rev'd Dr. Ernest C. Lucas

Vice-Principal Emeritus, Bristol Baptist College

Acknowledgments

I would like to acknowledge my debt to my longtime friend and co-author Roger Forster, with whom I first embarked on the adventure of writing theology and apologetics. I am grateful to all those over the years who gave endorsement or encouragement on earlier joint or solo works, including Rev. Dr. G. R. Beasley-Murray, Rev. Derek Kidner, Rev. G. W. Kirby, Rev. A. Morgan Derham, Prof. Leon Morris, Rev. Dr. A. Skevington-Wood, Prof. F. F. Bruce, Dr. Harold Ockenga, Rev. Dr. Nicky Gumbel, Prof. Gordon Wenham, Prof. Meic Pearse, Mr. Alan Storkey, Dr. Stephen Travis, Rev. Dr. Mark Bonnington, Rev. Dr. David Instone-Brewer, Rev. J. Allan Ellershaw, Prof. William Kay, Bishop David Roller, Rev. Prof. I. Howard Marshal, and Rev. Prof. Greg Boyd.

In 2018, I sent an early draft of the present work to my denominational Study Commission on Doctrine with the plea that they restore the biblical term "everlasting punishment" to our articles as they were in 1969, rather than its later replacement phrase "everlasting suffering" which is a non-biblical phrase and could be misleading. I am grateful for their kind and courteous response: that they noted the scholarly disagreement, and their reluctance to pursue it was more about the unlikely potential of adoption by the World Council than about the veracity of my argument. My thanks for encouragement and feedback as the work on the book progressed, from such as Ms. Jackie Pullinger-Toh, Prof. Paul Ewart, Prof. Malcolm Jeeves, Rev. Dr. Ernest Lucas, Rev. Prof. David Wilkinson, Dr. Nigel Wright, and more lately, Prof. Chris Date and

Rev. Prof. Kim Papaioannou. It is also much indebted to the more detailed works of Dr. Basil Atkinson, Rev. Dr. Edward Fudge, Rev. Dr. David Powys and Rev. Prof. Kim Papaioannou.

Abbreviations

Reference Works

NIDOTT	*New International Dictionary of Old Testament Theology*
NIDNTT	*New International Dictionary of New Testament Theology*
NT	New Testament
OT	Old Testament
TDNT	*Theological Dictionary of the New Testament*

Bible Versions

CSB	Christian Standard Bible
ESV	English Standard Version
JUB	Jubilee Bible
LXX	Septuagint
NET	New English Translation
NIV	New International Version
NKJV	New King James Version
NRSV	New Revised Standard Version
TLV	Tree of Life Version
WEB	Word English Bible
YLT	Young's Literal Translation

Abbreviations

Reference Works

Old Testament

Bible Versions

Introduction

I am grateful to be a long-standing lay minister in the evangelical Free Methodist Church (which now has a worldwide membership of over 1.5 million), and my previous Christian publications include a solo publication in Britain and the United States on the biblical teaching on the family, and several joint publications in both countries including the larger *Reason, Science and Faith* and *God's Strategy in Human History*, also published in the United States by Wipf and Stock.

I believe in the authority of Scripture, and like most evangelicals was brought up in a church that generally took Scripture to imply that the finally impenitent will suffer for unending time in "hell" without any hope of respite.

If this were really what Scripture taught, then we would either have to accept it as part of Christian belief, or conclude that Christianity is mistaken. But is it really what Scripture says? Or does the Bible consistently teach something quite different?

This is not a trivial issue. If eternal torment is true, then any people we have loved (friends, relatives, or indeed enemies), who have died without faith, face a horrendous fate. Surely, then, we should passionately want to check if it really *is* what Scripture teaches? Yet so many Christians seem to accept that "hell" means unending torment without any real study, sometimes seeming nervous to even question it in case they are thought theologically "unsound."

This present book seeks to summarize, for the general reader, why the scriptural passages on this issue simply do not teach any such horrendous doctrine. Hell (*Gehenna*) is real, and it was taught by Jesus himself, but we need to look at what he and his apostles actually say about hell and final judgment, and not rely on any unchecked church traditions.

The book invites you, therefore, to look with me at these passages, and form a careful conclusion as to what can and cannot be inferred from them.

Paul Marston

2023

1

The Basic Issues

Alternative Views of "Hell"

The New Testament (NT) clearly speaks of a day of judgment coming after a general resurrection, and says that the unrighteous will be judged. What will finally happen to them as a result of this judgment?

Four main suggestions have been made historically:

A. Unending Torment

"Eternal" means purely unending in time, and "eternal punishment" implies a *process* of torment in hell that is unending. Those who do not repent in this life will therefore suffer torment for unending time and without hope.

B. Destruction

"Eternal" is seen more as meaning "ultimate" or "for the age to come" and this applies to eternal life. The "age to come" or "eternal" punishment for the unrepentant is a painful process leading to a total destruction—a ceasing to exist that is permanent.

C. Hell with a Portal

In this view there is suffering in hell after the last judgment, but this can become corrective rather than punitive, and God's grace allows people there to repent and be restored.

D. Universalism

This is a version of the "portal" view where eventually everyone will be saved because God's love will prevail. Ultimately God will get what he wants, which is that none will be permanently lost.

So Which Is True?

All four have had advocates. The contention in the present book is that the consistent and repeated teaching in the New Testament is that the ultimate end of the determinedly unrepentant is destruction (implying ceasing to exist), and so this is the teaching of Jesus and his apostles. This may surprise some who have been taught that the Bible implies unending torment, and may think that to doubt it is to question the authority of Scripture. Yet in many cases they have simply assumed that this is the biblical teaching without any serious study. Does it really merit serious study?

The Importance of the Issue

This is not a trivial issue. This is not an issue about correct symbolism or nuances of theology. If unending torment is true, then this will be the horrendous fate of innumerable people (including many that we love). Many people suffer in this life but have hope, but this concerns unending suffering *without* hope. Surely this should make us concerned to examine very carefully what the Bible does teach on this issue? To do so is neither to "judge God" nor to doubt the New Testament but to make a serious effort to understand what it says.

Early Church and Evangelical Views

To evangelicals like the present author, the question of what Jesus taught is decided by study of the New Testament, not by human tradition. But assuredly, if a doctrine really is what the Bible teaches then at least some biblical scholars will have noted this—both in the early church and in recent times.

Universalism has not been common, though in the early church Gregory of Nyssa (and probably Origen) advocated it, and a recent work by Gregory MacDonald (Robin Parry), *The Evangelical Universalist*, also makes a case for it.

Destruction has had more support from theologically conservative biblical scholars. A similar view is sometimes called "annihilationism" or "conditionalism," but in this book the repeatedly used biblical term "destruction" is preferred—it is not an "ism." Two of the most important early church figures, Justin Martyr and Irenaeus of Gaul, taught it, and this is shown in a final chapter in this book. Over the last two hundred years many mainstream, Bible-believing Christian scholars, including a number prominent in the evangelical movement, have also held to this view. In the UK these include, e.g., Charles Gore, William Temple, Oliver Chase Quick, Basil Atkinson, H. Guillebaud, Ulrich Ernst Simon, John Wenham,[1] Michael Green, J. Stafford Wright, Norman Anderson, G. B. Caird, A. John Stott, W. Farrar, David Wilkinson, and Ernest Lucas. Others, e.g., J. Agar Beet, F. F. Bruce, R. T. France, I. Howard Marshall, and Ian Paul have shown sympathy, and Richard Bauckham and Graham Stanton and Steven Travis have commended books taking this view. Bruce wrote:

> Annihilation is certainly an acceptable interpretation of the relevant New Testament passages. . . . For myself, I remain agnostic. Eternal conscious torment is incompatible with the revealed nature of God.[2]

---

1. Some of the people here are referred to in Wenham, *Facing Hell*, 19.

2. Letter from F. F. Bruce to John Stott in 1989, as quoted in Dudley-Smith, *John Stott*, 354. In his preface to Fudge's book Bruce aligns with C. S. Lewis, who did not take a "traditional" view on hell but one resembling Wright's.

N. T. Wright rejects what he calls "conditionalism" but suggests that those who continue to reject God's love will ultimately become "creatures that still exist in an ex-human state."[3] This seems little different from ceasing to exist, so it could be taken as a kind of "portal" version of eventual destruction. In the United States, Joel Green has shown sympathy, and actual destruction advocates have included, e.g., Edward Fudge, Clarke Pinnock, E. Earl Ellis, and there are various other international scholars who accept it, some of whom contribute on the website www.rethinkinghell.com.

What seems surprising is that with so many well-known and scholarly theological conservatives and evangelicals recognizing that hell involves destruction, ordinary Bible-believing Christians often do not even consider it.

The works by Edward Fudge and David Powys are superb detailed biblical studies, but are very long books.[4] Kim Papaioannou's excellent *Geography of Hell* is 276 pages looking specifically at Jesus's teaching in the gospels. The present book is not intended to be innovative, nor as any contribution to academic scholarship, but to present the biblical teaching and evidence in a succinct and challenging way both to interested pastors and ordinary believers. In summary, the repeated and direct assertion in Scripture is that the ultimate end for the determinedly unrepentant is not unending torment but "destruction." This term "destruction," used in a judicial context, means a process leading to termination, ceasing to exist as an entity, and this is the most obvious and straightforward way to take the term as repeatedly used by the Bible in the context of hell and judgment. The result of God's "eternal judgment" is an "eternal punishment" which is "eternal destruction"— a process of finite duration leading to a cessation of existence that is permanent.

It has to be said that sometimes scholars seem to misrepresent what those of us who accept hell implies destruction actually believe, or seem to advocate unending torment based on rather

---

3. Wright, *Surprised by Hope*, 195. Greg Boyd in the United States seems to take a similar position.

4. Fudge, *Fire That Consumes,* is 417 pages, and Powys, *"Hell,"* is 478 pages.

casual reasoning. For example, Grant R. Osborne, admitting that some of the words in Revelation are interpretable in different ways, goes on to say:

> Repeated emphasis on eternal conscious torment in Jesus's teaching (Mark 9:48; Matt 3:12; 18:8; 25:41, 46, cf. the Gehenna imagery in Matt 5:22, 29–30; 10:28; 18:9; 23:15, 33 par) and in Revelation makes it unlikely it is merely a metaphor for ceasing to exist.[5]

But there is no such teaching in any of these references, and ceasing to exist must surely be the meaning in Rev 20:14?

John Nolland writes on Matt 5:29:

> "Destroy" would naturally imply annihilation. While there are no Matthean texts incompatible with such an understanding [footnote: The "eternal fire" of Mt 18:8; 25:42 can reasonably be taken as a fire that has been kept available (and will be kept available) for its destructive role] there is probably some early Jewish tradition of perpetual punishment, and some biblical texts are naturally read this way [footnote: Rev 14:11 is the most definite].[6]

As we will see, the appeal to contemporary Jewish context is to say the least shaky, and Revelation is not at all easy to interpret.

Finally, we will see later that G. K. Beale, in his very scholarly commentary on Revelation, seems to give too much notice to the supposed Jewish background (including the rather doubtful Neoplatonic late reworking of historical speeches in 4 Maccabees), in dismissing the understanding of hell as destruction.

The biblical arguments for hell (as Jesus taught) implying destruction need at least to be taken seriously.

Interpreting Scripture

Evangelical Christians believe that the only definite source of Christian doctrine is Scripture; but we have to rightly interpret

---

5. Osborne, *Revelation*, 548.
6. Nolland, *Gospel of Matthew*, 437.

it. One of the first things Jesus did after his resurrection was to "interpret" the Scriptures for the two on the road to Emmaus. The word used relates to our term "hermeneutics"—the principles of right interpretation of Scripture. So here are some well-established principles.[7]

Principle 1: Implicit Meaning

As with all language, there is implicit communication. Simple translation of words does not always convey meaning, which is why we need exegesis to understand what the words meant *to those who used them in the context in which they were used.*

Principle 2: Care with Words

Jesus spoke Aramaic, and the gospels are in Greek. We are not looking at transcripts but conveyance (as evangelicals we assume this to have been Spirit-guided) of *meaning* through translation. Sometimes words in one language are not easily translated into another. To take an example not connected with the present subject: the New Testament (NT) Greek word *gynē* can mean "wife" or "woman" and has no single English word to translate it. Also, some words can have a range of literal and metaphorical uses, or be used differently by different authors, but this does not imply that we can make them mean whatever we like.

Principle 3: Biblical Consistency

As evangelicals we will assume that there is a consistency between different scriptural passages because the same God is behind them. A "Jesus-centered" exegesis, of course, recognizes the power of "But I say unto you. . . ." The Old Testament (OT) sometimes laid down statutes embodying less than the ideal to which Jesus

---

7. There are various good books on this, e.g., Fee, *How to Read the Bible*, or the more detailed Klein, *Introduction to Biblical Interpretation.*

later called his disciples. Within the NT, however, we will expect a harmony in the thinking because Jesus is God's final word.

Principle 4: Care on Genre

Different parts of Scripture are prehistory, history, plain stated theology, poetry, literature, parable, and apocalyptic visions. We should be very wary of drawing doctrines from (say) poetry, parables or apocalyptic visions that are not clearly stated in the more prosaic theological passages.

Principle 5: Elements for Exegesis

There are several main elements needed for good exegesis:

The *"literary context"* is the determination of where a passage fits in the flow of thought of the writer—itself part of an overall structure.

The *"grammatical considerations,"* for most of us who are not fluent in the biblical languages, need to be taken on trust from commentaries by those who are. We have, of course, to remember that the Greek and Hebrew tense systems (so the experts tell us!) differ from ours. Good critical commentaries will tell us what possible meanings a particular sentence can have linguistically.

The *"historical-cultural context"* concerns the whole background of the writer, target group, occasion and purpose of writing, and the general culture. Without this, often the bare language does not convey the writer's real meaning. As already noted, there are often assumptions about the meanings of words that are related strongly to cultural context.

The aim in this book is to be careful in all this without being overcomplicated. It does not assume technical theological knowledge.

2

Word Studies

Soul/Life (Gk: *Psychē*)

This word came originally from a word for breath but came to include the conscious being and was much discussed by Greek philosophers. In the NT it can have a rich variety of meanings. It can simply mean physical life, or person, as, e.g., in John 13:37, Acts 15:26, and Acts 2:43. It can also mean "the inner life of man, equivalent to the ego, person, or personality, with the various powers of the soul."[1]

There were Greek philosophers who believed in human immortality but it was not in Jewish thinking. There is no indication in the NT that the soul/*psychē* is immortal. Immortality is not inherent, but a gift of God to those of faith who seek it (Rom 2:7; 1 Cor 15:42). James 5:20 tells us that "whoever brings back a sinner from wandering will save the sinner's soul from death" (NRSV). The *NIDNTT* notes, "The death from which it is said that the soul will be saved is eternal death, exclusion from eternal life."[2]

There was a change during the first two centuries as the older Jewish and Christian ideas about Hades and human mortality

---

1. G. Harder, in Brown, *NIDNTT*, 3:683.
2. G. Harder, in Brown, *NIDNTT*, 3:685.

8

were affected by Hellenistic ideas.[3] Elledge looks at various first-century Jewish works moving toward human immortality.[4] Usually, though, for Jews this was not inherent but dependent upon God. The first century Jewish philosopher Philo had a very complex view of the dualism of body and soul and is ambivalent on immortality in spite of his admiration for "the most holy Plato," who gave philosophical reasons to accept it![5] The Wisdom of Solomon is a first century BCE or CE. Alexandrian work and is critical of a hedonism based on the view that death means a person is "as though they have never been" (2:2). God created us for incorruption (2:23) and the righteous have a *hope of* immortality (3:4). Josephus, writing in the late first century, ascribed views on immortality to the Pharisees and Essenes, though this may be colored by a desire to render their ideas palatable in a Greco-Roman context. The late first or early second-century Neoplatonic 4 Maccabees we will look at later. There was also a move toward a less holistic and more dualistic view of the body and soul.[6]

The classic Jewish view, however, reflected in the NT, is that humans are not inherently immortal, and any continuing existence is dependent on God.

Hades/the Grave (Gk.: *Hades*)

So what happens to us immediately after we die?

The Old Testament View of Sheol/Hades

The Old Testament Hebrew concept of Sheol is the grave, and the Greek equivalent term is Hades, which is the term used in the LXX

3. Bauckham, *Fate of the Dead*, 34. There is a story of reversed fortunes in the Palestinian Talmud (y. Sank. 23c; y. Hag. 77d) which is written much later.

4. Elledge, *Resurrection of the Dead*, ch. 6. See also Papaioannou, *Geography of Hell*, 89–90.

5. Philo, *Quod Omnis Probus Liber Sit* 13. See Penner, "Philo's Eschatology," on Philo.

6. See Bauckham, *Fate*, 275.

Greek translation in common use in apostolic times. It is this Sheol connection, rather than the Greek myth ideas of the god Hades and his underworld, which underlie its biblical use. Both good and bad people go there, and it is consistently presented as a place of darkness and nothingness where God is not remembered (Job 10:21; 26:5; Ps 6:5; 30:9 [LXX 29:9]; 115:17 [LXX 113:25]; Prov 1:12; 27:20; Isa 5:14). In death there is no proclamation or praise (Ps 88:11 [LXX 29:9]; Isa 38:18). The psalmist describes the situation he sees for people after death:

> For in death there is no remembrance of you; in Sheol who can give you praise? (Ps 6:5 NRSV)

This seems the general view,[7] although God is present in Sheol (Ps 139:8).

The only record of someone coming back from Sheol is when a medium "calls up" Samuel (Sam 28:12). Here, "Why have you disturbed me?" could mean "Why have you awakened me from unconscious sleep?"; and we cannot even be sure it really was Samuel, given that spirits called by mediums are known to impersonate dead people.

So does the OT picture the nothingness of Sheol as the final end? Psalm 73:6 gives the hope of being with God "forever," but as noted below this is the same term as that used, e.g., in Exod 21:6 for someone being a human bondslave "forever." It is not necessarily literally forever. Psalm 49:15 and 16:10 can be read as a possible resurrection. In Ezek 37 is the famous passage about God re-embodying dry bones; Ezek 37:11–14 could imply that this was just a grisly metaphor about the return of Israel from captivity, but it could also be taken as an indication of personal resurrection. Likewise in Isaiah:

> Your dead shall live; their bodies shall rise. You who dwell in the dust, awake and sing for joy! For your dew is

---

7. My own view was arrived at independently, but Papaioannou reaches similar conclusions on Sheol/Hades in *Geography of Hell*, 89–90. His whole treatment of the term in 85–135 is excellent.

a dew of light, and the earth will give birth to the dead.
(Isa 26:10)

The most obvious OT allusion that from the nothingness of Sheol there will eventually be a general resurrection is in Daniel:

> The multitudes who sleep in the dust of the earth will awake: some to everlasting life, others to shame and everlasting contempt. (Dan 12:2 NIV)

This view of Sheol differs from many other cultures (e.g., Mesopotamians, Egyptians and Greeks) who had quite different ideas of what happens at death.[8] To the Greeks, Hades was both a place and a god and Greek and Roman figures like Orpheus, Odysseus, Psyche, Heracles, Alcestis, Aeneus, Theseus, and Hippolytus visited Hades. In various Orphic mystery cults Hades was a place initiates could visit. There were, of course, divergences in Greek views, and the Stoics and Epicureans Paul met in Athens did not believe in any afterlife, though differed on how life should be lived. In Plato's *Phaedo* Socrates is uncertain whether there is an afterlife or nothingness at death, but gives four reasons to believe the human soul is inherently immortal, and in the final part of Plato's *Republic* the hero Er visits Hades and when he comes back relates how good and bad behavior can lead to a range of fates in Hades: unending punishment (for the most evil people), or temporary punishment, or immediate bliss. None of these other views see Hades as a place where the dead await a general resurrection and final judgment. Zeus is just one player among others, not the one God who will finally administer justice.

Developments in Jewish Thought Pre-Jesus

So how did Jewish thought on Sheol/Hades develop up until the time of Jesus's ministry? There is voluminous and fascinating literature on this,[9] but here we need only a limited summary.

8. See, e.g., Bauckham, *Fate*, and Longenecker, *Life in the Face of Death*.

9. See, e.g., Longenecker, *Life in the Face of Death*, and Elledge, *Resurrection of the Dead*, for many references.

The book of 1 Enoch was a Jewish work in five or six different sections; the first (11–36) was written during the third century BCE and the rest before Jesus's birth.[10] References to it in Jude 6, and actual quotation in Jude 14–15 are well analyzed by Richard Bauckham.[11] Protestants, Catholics, and most Orthodox churches exclude it from Scripture, its apocalyptic style makes it hard to determine how much was intended as literal, and it is sometimes contradictory—the later written introduction in 1:2 presents it as a vision and a parable. The many commentaries on it cannot be summarized, but at this point we are just asking what it says about experiences in Sheol. Nickelsburg explains that Mesopotamian influences are possible, but it seems likely that

> the Enoch cosmology reflects contemporary Greek sources. Moreover, the accounts of Enoch's journeys appear to be modelled not on the Gilgamesh epic but on Greek Nekyias, accounts of visits of the underworld found in Homer, Plato and Plutrarch. . . . Greek mythology appears also to have left its imprint in 1 Enoch.[12]

Nickelsburg further suggests that the separation of souls after death may be beholden to Orphic myths. So the souls are put into one of four "hollows" (22:2ab), or is it three (22:9a)? Either just three are dark and one illuminated with a spring of water, or all four are dark (22:2c). Nickelsburg explains:

> A compartment for the righteous: vv 10–11, a compartment where sinners who were not recompensed on earth are punished: vv 12–13, a compartment for sinners whose violent deaths resulted in less, or no, punishment for them after death.[13]

---

10. See Nickelsburg, *1 Enoch*, and Nickelsburg, *Commentary on the Book of Enoch*. Nickelsburg's translation is quoted in this book, but the earlier one of Charles is very similar.

11. Bauckham, *Jude, 2 Peter*, 51–53, 94–97.

12. Nickelsburg, *Commentary on 1 Enoch*, 62.

13. Nickelsburg, *Commentary on 1 Enoch*, 303.

The description is a bit confused, and the sufferings of the sinners in their hollow are only until the day of judgment. But the hollow for the righteous can hardly be called "paradise," the body-soul dualism is Greek, and the whole scene is one from Greek mythology not Hebrew thinking on Sheol. The early part of the book describes a kind of paradise garden with symbolic trees, including the one which led to expulsion from Eden (25–32), but "no mortal is permitted to touch it till the great judgment" (25:4). This resembles that garden in Rev 22 which is likewise not a present paradise but a post-judgment one. Elledge notes, however, that a bodily resurrection is only hinted at and not specified, and that after "the day" the righteous will not literally live forever but will have "prolific longevity and myriad offspring."[14] This is in marked contrast to Jesus in Luke 20:35, etc.

In other pre-Jesus Jewish sources, the coming "day of judgment" also features, but not the picture of a Greek-like Sheol. In the Psalms of Solomon (ca. second or first century BCE) the destruction of the sinner is forever, but "they that fear the Lord shall rise to life eternal" (3:16). In 2 Maccabees (a second-century BCE work) the hero looks forward to resurrection to life but warns the tyrant that there will be no such resurrection for him (7:9). For those who "fall asleep in godliness" there is an expectation that they will rise again (12:44). Elledge gives a careful analysis of the idea of resurrection in the various Dead Sea Scrolls, and concludes that, although rare, there were multiple references in their later literature.[15]

There were afterlife deniers: the early second-century BCE *Wisdom of Ben Sirach* was written by an Egyptian Jew and says nothing about the day of judgment, but that in Hades no one will sing the praises of the Lord "as from one who does not exist, thanksgiving has ceased." However, Bauckham says that Ben Sira

---

14. Elledge, *Resurrection of the Dead*, 133.

15. Elledge, *Resurrection of the Dead*, 173.

is probably the last Jewish writer of the Second Temple period of whom it can be confidently stated that he did not expect life and judgment after death.[16]

Bauckham notes that the Sadducees were differentiated from the Pharisees because of their disbelief in the resurrection, but that most other contemporary Jews also believed in the resurrection. N. T. Wright also asserts:

> Resurrection was not simply a doctrine of the Pharisees
> . . . with the few exceptions noted it was widely believed
> by most Jews around the turn of the common era.[17]

The book 1 Enoch, with its vision of Hades, may have been known, but there seem no references to suggest that death was seen other than a sleep to await the resurrection.

At the same time, the Jewish Diaspora were spread widely. There were Jewish communities in Babylon and in Egypt (Alexandria); and the apostle Paul, who was a "Hebrew of the Hebrews" (Phil 3:5), could quote Greek poets in Athens. Other cultures' stories about visits to Hades were likely known in folklore.

New Testament Teaching

The NT routinely refers to death as falling asleep (Matt 27:52; Acts 7:6; 13:36; 1 Cor 15:18; 15:20; 1 Thess 4:13; 4:15; 2 Pet 3:4). John 11:11–13 illustrates that there is a word for "death" that is different from that for "sleep," but death is seen as a kind of sleep—presumably like natural sleep but permanent (at least until there is a resurrection). The popular idea that good people die and go straight to "heaven" is not taught in the NT.

Paul says that he was brought up to believe like other Pharisees in the resurrection, which he takes to be of both the just and the unjust (Acts 23:6; 23:8; 24:15; 24:21). In John 11:25 Martha affirms the belief that "in the last day" her dead brother will rise

16. Bauckham, in Longenecker, *Life in the Face of Death*, 82.
17. Wright, *Resurrection of the Son of God*, 147.

again; she does *not* say that she is happy because she knows he is now in paradise or in the bosom of Abraham. All this is consistent with the belief that in Hades there is no consciousness as everyone awaits the resurrection and the last judgment in "the Day" (Matt 10:15; 11:22; 11:24; Matt 12:35; Acts 17:31; Rom 2:16; 2 Pet 2:9; 2 Pet 3:7; 1 John 4:17).

The official Roman Catholic catechism asserts that the NT speaks of judgment "primarily" in terms of the second coming, but claims that the NT "repeatedly affirms each will be rewarded immediately after death in accordance with his works and faith."[18] It says "repeatedly affirms" but cites only the words to the criminal on the cross and the parable of the rich man and Lazarus. Two other verses (both irrelevant) are sometimes also cited. First Peter 3:19 says that Jesus, being made alive by the Spirit, "went to preach to the spirits in prison"—but 2 Pet 2:4 makes it clear these prisoners are fallen angels in Tartarus, not humans in Hades. The other misused verse is Eph 4:9, which cites Ps 68, and adds, "In saying 'he ascended,' what does it mean but that he had also descended into the lower regions, the earth?" But the point is that he descended to earth (as in John 3:13) not to Hades, and as he ascended to heaven he led a triumphant train of living Christian "captives" (as in 2 Cor 2:14), from which he gave the church gifts of (living Christian) apostles, evangelists, etc. It is clearly *not* about some supposed visit to dead believers in Hades.

The NT gives no indication that people exist as disembodied spirits after death,[19] and gives no other point for the divine judgment after death other than at the "last day" or "final judgment," which is portrayed as a very public event. Paul tells the Thessalonians that he would not have them uninformed of the situation of believers who have "fallen asleep," but his assurance is not that these are in paradise (or purgatory) but that their cessation is not permanent because they await the resurrection (1 Thess 4:13–18). Jesus's resurrection assures this, and otherwise their cessation of existence would be permanent (1 Cor 15:12–28).

---

18. See https://www.usccb.org/sites/default/files/flipbooks/catechism/268.

19. Luke 8:15 just means the girl started breathing.

Hades is referred to nine times in Revelation (at which we will look later), and elsewhere only five times in the NT. Matthew 11:15 and Luke 10:15 refer to Capernaum being "brought down to Hades," which in context refers to the destruction of the cities to which it is compared. In Acts 2:27 and 2:31 it refers to the *psychē* of Jesus not being left in Hades (i.e., dead) but being resurrected. In Matt 16:18 Jesus says he will build his church and "the Gates of Hades will not prevail against it,"—a shot at a local Banias Pan-worship cave, and also to say that death/hades would be defeated.

The one passage that stands out as different is the story Jesus told about the rich man and Lazarus in Hades. Some of his hearers may well have known of the 1 Enoch stories, of Plato's story of Er, or of stories in the Orphic mystery cults. An Egyptian demotic text dating soon after Jesus gave a story of a much earlier visit to the realm of the dead by a reincarnated magician, Si-osiris.[20] We have no evidence that there were Jewish schools of theology at this time who believed in an orphic-type Hades, but who knows what some of the "Jews in the street" thought? Many in society and churches today believe that good people "go straight to heaven" when they die, even though the NT says they will await resurrection and judgment.

So does Jesus really intend to confirm that an orphic-type Hades is an accurate picture of what happens after death?

The first thing to note is that Jesus often begins a parable without identifying it as such. In Luke 15:11, e.g., he begins: "A certain man had two sons . . ." and gives the parable of the prodigal and the elder son. Likewise for the parable of the corrupt steward in Luke 16:1–8. It has sometimes been suggested that Luke 16:19–31 is not a parable because Jesus gives a specific name Lazarus. This misses the point that the name "Lazarus" is another form of "Eliezer," Abraham's steward who obtained a bride for Isaac—so who more natural to fly to his side and be entrusted with a message back to earth? The story is a parable.

---

20. See Papaioannou, *Geography of Hell*, 116, and Bauckham, *Parallels*, 226. A much later story in the Talmud also speaks of a weighing of good and bad deeds determining bliss or suffering in Hades as seen in a visit.

A second point is that any justice system that put suspects under torture before their trial should surely be condemned? If the rich man was awaiting trial at the last judgment then why was he being tormented? "Shall not," this same Abraham asked in confidence that the answer would be affirmative, "the judge of all the earth do right?" (Gen 18:25). The Roman Catholics, as noted, get around this by suggesting the judgment is at death, but in this case why the repeated emphasis in the NT of the day of judgment if the sentences are already given? What would be the point?

With a parable, moreover, it is important to ascertain the point or points it is making, and not stretch it to other issues. Craig Blomberg sees this as a "three-point parable," but warns:

> The restrictions against unlimited allegorizing and the fact that the source for much of the imagery was popular folklore should warn against viewing the details of this narrative as a realistic description of the afterlife.[21]

We are not told why there was this reversal of fortunes, but it seems unlikely that it was just some kind of balancing-out process. Abraham reminds him that he had a good time in his lifetime, but does not say this was the *cause* of his present distress. It is not money but *love of money* that is the root of evil (1 Tim 6:1), and Abraham himself was wealthy. There is nothing wrong with being rich, but the Lukan literary context is all about love of money associated with selfishness. In Luke 12:15 Jesus warns about greed. He goes on to tell the story of the rich fool whose only thought was to live in luxury with no thought for anyone else. It was not his business success but his selfishness that was the issue. In Luke 14:12–14 Jesus does not tell them to become paupers, but that they should invite the poor and crippled to come and eat with them and not just other rich people who will issue return invites. This is the context of Luke 14:33 when he says they have to renounce all to follow him. Luke 16:1–9 says they should use their wealth well. In Luke 16:11–13 there is more about God and money and

---

21. Blomberg, *Parables*, 260. See also, e.g., Wenham, *Parables of Jesus*, and others.

that someone cannot serve both. In 16:14 the Pharisees ridiculed him because they were "lovers of money," and many of them were selfish, cared for no one else, and were serving money not God. Jesus reasserts the truth of the Law and the Prophets, and then there is a very brief discussion on divorce, maybe (as in Matt 19) in response to a question about the Law on this. But then he goes immediately into the parable of the rich man and Lazarus. The rich man asked for Lazarus to go and tell his brothers to "repent," surely not of being rich but of being selfish? When Jesus says that they have the Law and the Prophets, the implication is that they have ignored the demands by the prophets for compassion and care for the poor—as well as rejecting the Messiah prophesied by them.

We may see this as background, but it is surely not the main point of the story. Nor is the story aimed at scaring the unrepentant Pharisees. They have ignored a whole series of warnings about their fate at the last judgment (in which they believed), so why try to scare them with a story about torment in Hades when there is no evidence they believed in this? The phrase "the bosom of Abraham" appears nowhere in pre-Jesus Jewish literature, and Jews did not believe that righteous souls were wafted off there at death.[22] It seems logical to conclude that Jesus is not attacking some established theological view of Hades, but reacting to popular folklore.[23] When in Matt 10:16 he tells them to be as "wise as serpents" he is not teaching biology (snakes are comparatively stupid) but using popular folklore to make a point. The story may be *about* people like the self-centered Pharisees, but is not aimed *at* them. The real point of the parable is its climax. Some may have asked why God could not send some dramatic proof to those who claimed to follow God but who rejected Jesus and his teaching; in particular, why not send someone back from Hades as popular folk stories suggested? The answer is that it wouldn't work.

22. Nolland, *Luke 9:21—18:34*, 832, also points out this was not the normal expectation for pious Jews.

23. Marshall in *Luke*, 637, suggested an extrabiblical influence, and the reference to popular folklore expanded, e.g., in Bauckham, *Parables*, and Papaioannou, *Geography of Hell*, 112, etc.

The idea of a split Sheol/Hades with a chasm between appears absolutely nowhere else in Scripture, and Papaioannou (whose analysis on all this is excellent) plausibly concludes:

> The parable functions as a parody on popular tales about communication with the dead and as such should not be used to color the understanding of Luke's use of Hades.[24]

Jesus's story is parody, hyperbole to the point of satire. None of the folklore stories, Orphic myths, or 1 Enoch have a picture like this, and it is a caricature.[25] It is not a visionary visit there and back from a seer/prophet, nor a visit there and back from a hero like Er or Odysseus. Hades is split neatly into two parts, and if an obscure rich man could argue with Abraham, then presumably lots of friends and relatives are talking and arguing with each other across the great chasm. Some who are in the bosom of an ancient nomadic sheikh may be having to refuse requests for help from close relatives in agonising pain. The rich man, in Jesus's satire, is not screaming for mercy from God (having realized his mistake) but still trying to make capital from his descent from Abraham (see Luke 3:8) and Abraham recognizes the man as his "child" but says he cannot help. The rich man asks for just a tiny drop of water but what use would this be in a raging inferno? His next suggestion is that Lazarus should return from Hades to warn people. But in 1 Enoch, the Hades visit was by a recognized, exalted figure, Enoch; in Plato's story, Er of Pamphylia is a known soldier hero; and in the Egyptian story, it is the reincarnated magician Si-osiris. But if Lazarus went back in a recognizably sore-infested, ragged state, why would anyone believe he had really been in Hades? And if it were as an unembodied spirit, why would this carry credibility with those who thought Jesus in league with evil forces and believed that the dead were asleep awaiting the resurrection? It is an absurd idea. So Jesus makes the basic point. The Law and the Prophets both demand compassion for the poor and foretell the

---

24. Papaioannou, *Geography of Hell*, 135.

25. Papaioannou also points out the differences between the "geography" in the parable and 1 Enoch in *Geography of Hell*, 118.

kind of ministry he has been doing as signs that he is the Messiah, so if they don't choose to listen to this then nothing will convince them. We know all too well today how people can cling to inconsistent beliefs in the face of all evidence. Jesus also used satire in saying that it is easier for a camel to go through the eye of a needle than a rich man to enter the kingdom (Luke 24:25). His hearers then seem (to use a non-theological term) to be gobsmacked, and he ironically remarks that human impossibilities are possible with God. But if this kind of satire is his purpose, then the Hades scene is no more intended to reflect reality than the talking animals in Aesop's parables, or the scenes in Dickens's famous extended parable about ghosts and spirits in *A Christmas Carol*. It is a skit on popular folklore stories, not an attack based on any established theological system, because there was none.

Is it prophetic or coincidence that sometime later a man called Lazarus *did* come back from Hades (John 11)? Did he come back having had a tour, or from spending time in some paradisical part of Hades? Was he pressed with questions about what Hades was like? Jesus says that Lazarus has "fallen asleep" (John 11:11), meaning he is dead (11:14). He does not say that Lazarus is temporarily in some kind of Hades paradise, and the natural reading would be that Lazarus was not conscious and would have no Hades-tour story to recount on his return. John 11:45–48; 12:9–11 says that his resurrection brought many to faith, but surely because of the miracle not because of any tales of Hades he brought back.

This is relevant to an incident when, on the cross, Jesus told the criminal: "I tell you today you will be with me in paradise" (Luke 23:43). The Greek contains no punctuation indication, so it could mean "I tell you today that you will be with me in paradise" or "I tell you that today you will be with me in paradise." In the absence of the word "that" (*hoti*) it could mean either. The word "paradise" is a borrowed Persian word for garden, and appears in the NT elsewhere only in 2 Cor 12:4 and Rev 2:7. Does it mean some idyllic part of Hades? The term could hardly be used to describe the very basic amenities in the section of Hades for the righteous in 1 Enoch, and there is no indication that it was used in this way by any Jews before Jesus. The paradise in Rev 2:7 is a vision of the future after the day of judgment (and many take it to be a restoration of the "paradise" lost in Eden). We don't know why the criminal was executed by Rome, and the fact that he says, "This man has done nothing wrong," may indicate that he knew about Jesus and may even have been a follower. He asks, "Remember me when you come into your kingdom." Did Jesus "come into his kingdom" the day he died? Most take it that he either came into his kingdom the day of his resurrection (three days later) or will do at the *parousia*. But it would surely not mean the "today" when the request was made? So surely the promise of "paradise" could not literally mean that it would happen in that twenty-four hours and before the resurrection? Jesus made the promise "today" but did not say when the paradise promise would be fulfilled.

The man "caught up" to paradise in 1 Cor 12:4 may simply have had a vision, as John did in Revelation, of the post-parousia new age. There is no reason to believe the paradise is there *now*, any more than the New Jerusalem and its waters and tree of life.

If, as suggested, the dead are simply unconscious, this would explain also Paul saying in Phil 1:23 that he is torn between remaining in the body or "to depart and be with Christ." He does not say "to depart for paradise," and his words could quite naturally mean that he expects as he enters the sleep of death that the next thing of which he will be aware is the resurrection to eternal life. He does not say in 1 Thess 4:15–18 that those who have "fallen asleep" are now in paradise with Jesus, but that they await the resurrection—and then will "always be with the Lord."

This seems the most natural way to understand the New Testament teaching on what happens after death. Bauckham notes the apparent change in Jewish and Christian thinking during the first two centuries from this older view of Hades to a belief that judgment would begin immediately after death.[26] With increasing Hellenization of theology, later writers (Christian and Jewish) may have seen Hades as a final place of reward or unending punishment. But, for those of us who believe the New Testament, Hades

---

26. Bauckham, *Fate of the Dead*, 34.

is the place where people await the resurrection and final judgment. It seems most likely that the dead are simply unconscious.

In Revelation, as we shall see, Hades becomes, as in Greek mythology, both a place and an individual (at one point following Death riding a horse) which/who is destroyed in the lake of fire. But this is metaphorical apocalyptic, not literal description. Nowhere else in the Bible is Hades presented as such a place.

Just as a final point, it should be noted that whatever is decided about the meaning of this parable, it cannot affect the fact that in Hades people await the resurrection and final judgment. It does not tell us what will happen at that time to the determinedly unrepentant. Whether they are conscious or unconscious in the meantime cannot imply what happens post-final-judgment.

Torment (Gk: *Basanos*)

The *New International Dictionary of New Testament Theology* (*NIDNTT*) says the term originally meant a testing, then torture as a means of examination, and finally torment generally.[27] The verb can mean to torment or oppress, or describe continuing mental anguish as Lot was tormented by the evil around him (2 Pet 2:8). In 4 Maccabees it is used many times for a tyrant who tortures captives to death, but also in 9:32 to tell the tyrant "you suffer torment by the threats that come from impiety."

Are the unrighteous eventually to suffer *unending* torment?

The verbal or noun forms of the term are used twenty-one times in the NT. There is no mention of humans suffering future torment as a result of sin in Matthew, Mark, John's gospel or letters, Hebrews, Acts, any of Paul's writings, Peter, or James. In Rev 20:10 the devil will be tormented, but his followers just consumed. Babylon is said to suffer torment (18:7, 10, 15), though this seems to be temporary. In Rev 9:1–11 there is a temporary time of human torment from scorpion-like stings. The only other place where humans suffer judgmental torment is the worshippers of the beast in

27. W. Mundle, in Brown, *NIDNTT*, 3:855–56.

Rev 14:10–11, a passage which we will look at below. In the parable of the rich man and Lazarus there is the reference to suffering torment in Hades, but we have seen that this is no basis on which to decide what is the final fate of anyone after the resurrection and judgment—even if it were to tell us anything about the intermediate state in the grave.

The phrase "eternal torment" is never applied to humans anywhere in Scripture, so why do so many Bible-believing Christians and churches adopt the phrase?

Destruction/Destroy/Perish (Gk: *Apōleia, Apollymi*)

This, in its various forms, is really a key term in the issue, so we need to look at it more carefully. The debate is whether in the context of a judicial act this term really means "destroy" or "make to suffer for unending time without hope."

Its use in the Septuagint (LXX), the standard Greek translation of the OT in apostolic times, is relevant. The *NIDNTT* states:

> In the LXX *apollymi* represents 38 different Heb. words. Most frequently it stands for *'ābad*, to be lost, perish or destroy. In non-religious contexts it is used variously of the destruction of a city, a group of people, or a tribe (cf. Num 16:33; 32:39; 33:53) . . . *Apollymi* (often used in the active) threatens the very existence of an individual or group such as one's enemies. Of great importance are the requirements of the Holiness Code. These were transgressions of the Law such as those who make child sacrifice to Moloch and those who consult fortune tellers or spirits of the dead, and they will be "cut off" from the people of the covenant. In other words they will be stoned (Lev 20:3, 5, 6). The exhortations which conclude the book of Deuteronomy confront the whole nation with the alternative of receiving a long life by means of obedience, or the curse of extinction by disobedience. (Deut 28:20, 22, 24; 30:18 *etc*). Thus *apōleia* involves not

only exclusion from belonging to Yahweh, but also destruction and loss of life.[28]

Typical of its use is the LXX of Gen 19:12–13:

Then the men said to Lot, "Have you anyone here, in-laws or sons or daughters? Or if you have anyone else in the city, bring them out of this place. For we are about to destroy (*apollymen*) this place because the outcry concerning them has been raised before the Lord, and the Lord has sent us to obliterate it."

The fire and brimstone totally obliterated Sodom. The word "obliterate" is *ektribontes*, and *apollymen* is seen as meaning the same thing here.

Jesus uses the same terms:

On the day when Lot went out from Sodom, fire and sulfur rained from heaven and destroyed (*apōlesen*) them all. (Luke 17:29 ESV)

There is no concept of any continued suffering, nor of just being in a poor kind of existence; the city and the people have totally ceased to exist as entities. The total emptiness of the wasteland is noted, e.g., in Zeph 2:9, and was talked of even by Jews in the first century.

The consistent biblical meaning of "destroy," applied in a judgmental context to cities or people, means they cease to exist as entities. If there is any suffering involved it is in the process of reaching that point of nonexistence. In Obad 1:15–16 the "day of the Lord" will make the nations opposed to God "*as though they had never been*," and 1:18 refers to Edom being burned and destroyed like stubble. How could annihilation/destruction be more clearly stated? Malachi 4:1–3 likewise seems to say that the wicked will be "burned up," leaving nothing but "ashes under the soles of your feet, on the day when I act, says the Lord of hosts."

---

28. H. C. Hahn, in Brown, *NIDNTT*, 1:463–64.

In general, when the term is used in judgment, it seems to imply obliteration rather than leaving in a state of prolonged pain. Thus in Jesus's parables:

> They said to Him, "He will *destroy* those wicked men miserably, and lease his vineyard to other vinedressers." (Matt 21:41 NKJV)

> The king was enraged. He sent his troops, *destroyed* those murderers, and burned their city. (Matt 22:7 NRSV)

The implication is that they were to be killed, and the ESV translates Matt 21:41 explicitly as having this meaning. In 1 Cor 10:5 it refers to those *destroyed* by serpents, again meaning those killed.

When used to indicate a deliberate wrong act toward someone it has the same meaning of terminating their life. Matthew 2:13 tells us that Herod wanted to search for the child (Jesus) to *destroy* him—to kill him. The Pharisees and Herodians wanted to *destroy* Jesus (Mark 3:6), the chief priests and the scribes were seeking a way to *destroy* (*apolesōsin*) him (Mark 11:18), and later the chief priests and the elders persuaded the crowd to ask for Barabbas and *destroy* (*apolesōsin*) Jesus (Matt 27:20)—in this latter case specifically asking for death by crucifixion.

One argument sometimes used is that death is not really a termination of existence because people have immortal souls, and so just enter a new state. However, the chief priests were Sadducees and definitely did not believe in immortal souls—as far as they were concerned it was a permanent obliteration, and quite likely when Herod sought to "destroy" the baby messiah then as far as he was concerned it was termination. Obadiah (as we saw above) specifically saw judicial destruction as ultimately leaving the wicked "as though they had never existed."

The parallel term "to perish" (also from *apollymi*) generally means to have a violent death (e.g., Matt 8:25; Matt 26:52; Luke 11:51; Luke 13:3, 5; Acts 5:37; Heb 11:31; 2 Pet 3:6, 9; Jude 11).

Paul, in one place, *contrasts* suffering with destruction:

> . . . persecuted, but not forsaken; struck down, but not
> *destroyed.* (2 Cor 4:9 ESV)

In numerous biblical references there is no instance in which to "destroy" someone means to put them in prolonged suffering or to "perish" means to be in a deliberately arranged prolonged suffering, let alone an unending one.

As we will see, throughout the NT the ultimate end of the determinedly unrepentant will be to "perish" and be "destroyed." So how has this come to be interpreted by so many as being put in an unending state of torment without hope?

We know now, of course, that the laws of conservation of mass-energy imply that the actual physical elements still exist when a city or person is "destroyed." But Obadiah or the chief priests were not interested in nuclear physics, and in general terms we say that a city or person "no longer exists" when it or they cease to exist as any kind of functional entity. Jesus remarks that actions which lead to split wineskins destroy them (Matt 9:17)—they no longer function as wineskins. In Mark 14:4 (and Matt 26:8) a woman breaks a jar of nard and pours it on Jesus's head. The perfume jar was destroyed and ceased to exist as a potential sale item, and the disciples asked, "Why this destruction?" But it was not an act of judicial judgment, and the woman did not put the jar or the nard in a state of prolonged suffering. It is bizarre to use these nonjudgmental "destructions" of inanimate objects to argue, as some have, that judicial destruction of humans in the age to come involves unending suffering.

Sometimes the Greek term *destroy/perish* is rendered "lose." Could this indicate some kind of unending tormented existence? We will now consider verses about which this is sometimes argued.

One place where many versions render it "lose" is when Jesus says:

> And if your right eye causes you to stumble, gouge it
> out, and throw it away! It is better for you that one part
> of your body should be *destroyed*, than that your whole
> body be thrown into Gehenna. (Matt 5:29 TLV)

But an eye gouged out and thrown away does not continue in some kind of tortured existence; in any real sense it ceases to exist as any kind of functional entity.

Another verse sometimes rendered "lose" is:

> And whoever gives one of these little ones even a cup of cold water because he is a disciple, truly, I say to you, he will by no means *lose* his reward. (Matt 10:42 ESV)

To "lose" (*apolesē*) a reward here means it is "lost" in a sense of not existing, it does not imply some kind of tortured existence.

There is one unusual sense in which the term is used (in several places) to mean to give up to death:

> Whoever would save his life (*psychēn*) will lose it, but whoever *loses* his life (*psychēn*) for my sake will find it. (Matt 16:25 ESV)

This verse is generally seen as a play on the two different meanings of *psychē*: preserving one's physical life from destruction could be at the expense of losing one's true self.[29]

The term can be also used metaphorically in other senses.

Jesus tells us the story of the sheep, which had "gone astray" (*planēthē*), for which the shepherd searches, and adds:

> So it is not the will of my Father who is in heaven that one of these little ones should perish (*apolētai*). (Matt 18:14 ESV)

Luke, however, uses different language for this parable and a similar parable, and dramatizes it. In Luke 15:4–10 the man has lost (*apolesas*) a sheep and then finds it, and a woman loses (*apolesē*) a coin. Here the sheep and coin were not, of course, "destroyed" in any literal sense—though neither were they in prolonged suffering and nor was it a permanent state. Jesus explains that the shepherd was concerned the sheep might perish (die), but for all we know the sheep itself may well have been quite happy, not realizing it was "lost," and the coin knew nothing about it. Neither sheep nor coin

---

29. See, e.g., G. Harder, in Brown, *NIDNTT*, 3:683, or France, *Gospel of Matthew*, 399n4.

were damaged or suffering, and in neither case is it the result of a purposeful act of judgment—shepherds do not intentionally "lose" sheep nor women coins. This contrasts sharply with the use of the term as an act of conscious judgment by God (or mis-judgment by Herod). It is a big stretch from the passive use of the term in these parables to suggest that the term, when used judicially, could mean causing unending suffering.

The metaphorical use of the term is also illustrated in the story of the prodigal son in Luke 15:17–32. Here the father says that the son was *lost* (*apolōlōs*), and is found, but also says that he was *dead*, and is now alive again. Plainly the son was *not* dead (though he feared he was "going to perish" [*apollymai*] of hunger) but was dead *to the father*. Neither the term "lost" nor the term "dead" would naturally in this context imply prolonged suffering. The son was "lost" and "dead" *to the father* even when he was having a good time.

The lost sheep, lost coin, and lost (or dead) son are not lost because of a judicial act made by the shepherd, woman or father, and their situation is temporary. None of the verses imply permanent or prolonged torment, so why should these unusual metaphorical uses subvert the very general meaning of the term—which whenever it is used of an active judgment means simply to "destroy."

It was once suggested to me that a kind of permanent state of lostness could be seen in Matt 7:

> Enter by the narrow gate. For the gate is wide and the way is easy that leads to destruction, and those who enter by it are many. For the gate is narrow and the way is hard that leads to life, and those who find it are few. (Matt 7:13–14 ESV)

This, however, simply says that the bad choice is a path that "leads to" destruction, it does not imply that destruction itself is a permanent state of suffering.

Interestingly Paul in 1 Corinthians says:

> But if there is no resurrection of the dead, then not even Christ has been raised. And if Christ has not been raised,

then our preaching is in vain and your faith is in vain. We are even found to be misrepresenting God, because we testified about God that he raised Christ, whom he did not raise if it is true that the dead are not raised. For if the dead are not raised, not even Christ has been raised. And if Christ has not been raised, your faith is futile, and you are still in your sins. Then those also who have fallen asleep in Christ have perished (*apōlonto*). (1 Cor 15:13–18 ESV)

Does Paul mean to imply that if there is no resurrection then dead Christians are suffering torment without end in a hell? Surely not? To Paul, the Messiah died for our sins, but our resurrected life is tied up with his resurrection. Without this, Christians would have "perished" in the sense of having ceased permanently to exist. Then we might as well say, "Eat, drink, and be merry for tomorrow we die!" Those who say this believe death is extinction, not that it is suffering for unlimited time. Powys comments that this passage has "a strong suggestion that the fate of the unrighteous may be destruction."[30] Surely Paul doesn't mean that they must have "perished" in the sense of being in unending torment? The time he is referring to is in any case now, *before* any resurrection to the final judgment.

If there is no resurrection, Paul implies, then dead Christians have not merely "perished" in the physical sense but their very beings or *psychēs* have been permanently terminated and ceased to exist. The repeated assertion in the NT (as we note below) is that the final end of the determinedly unrepentant is to be *destroyed* or *perish*—this is most naturally taken to mean that they will cease to exist.

30. Powys, "Hell," 280.

Eternal (Gk: *Aiōnios*)

The meaning of this term is complex.[31] An important background to it is the Hebrew term *ŏlam*, which means a long time, lifetime, or an age.

Tomasino, in the *New International Dictionary of Old Testament Theology & Exegesis* (*NIDOTT*), says of this:

> It does not seem to mean eternity in the philosophical sense of the word (i.e., neither unbounded time nor eternal timelessness) although there are a few vv. where the meaning . . . is very much like the idea of eternity.[32]

The LXX Greek version of the Old Testament in common use by first-century Jews usually translates *ŏlam* into the Greek *aiōn*. The base meaning of this is an "age," and the adjective *aiōnios* derives from this. In some cases it means in a lifetime (e.g., Deut 15:17; Exod 21:6; 1 Chr 28:4). Things relating to the Old Covenant are said to be *aiōnion* (Exod 12:14; 29:9; Num 10:8; 15:15; 1 Chr 23:13), yet in Heb 8:13 it says the old covenant is becoming obsolete and ready to vanish away. So it is not literally unending.

When used of the future, *ŏlam* "can refer to a future of limited duration."[33] For example, a slave could choose to remain with his master *ŏlam*, meaning permanently (and compare Phlm 15). In 1 Sam 1:22 Hannah vows that her child will remain in the house of God at Shiloh *'ad ŏlam*, meaning for the rest of his life (the LXX uses *aiōnos* here). The earth is established "forever" (Eccl 1:4), and Solomon hopes that God will dwell in his temple "forever" (1 Kgs 8:13).

This, then, probably colors the NT use of *aiōn/aiōnios*. Thus there are many references to the "present age" or "present world" (e.g., 1 Tim 6:17; Tit 2:12; Matt 13:32; Mark 4:19; Luke 16:8; 1 Cor 1:20), and to the "end of the age" (e.g., Matt 13:49; 28:20). This

---

31. Papaioannou, *Geography of Hell*, 41–48, contains a detailed look at this.

32. A. Tomasino, in VanGemeren, *NIDOTT*, 3:346.

33. A. Tomasino, in VanGemeren, *NIDOTT*, 3:347.

age is compared to the age to come where, e.g., followers making sacrifices for Jesus will receive

> a hundredfold now in this age (*aiōn*)—houses and brothers and sisters and mothers and children and lands, with persecutions—and in the age (*aiōni*) to come, eternal (*aiōnion*) life. (Mark 10:30 NRSV)[34]

At one time it was common to suppose that *aiōnios* simply meant unending time. However, Papaioannou rightly notes:

> A growing number of commentators are convinced that the adjective (*aiōnios*) conveys a more varied meaning. While it may have referred to long periods of time, in many instances in the New Testament it has been influenced by the theology of the two ages and therefore has come to mean, "pertaining to the age to come." In such usages, the quantitative aspect recedes into the background and the word takes on a strongly qualitative color.[35]

He later concludes that the adjective *eternal*

> refers primarily to things that pertain to the coming age thus having a qualitative emphasis, while at the same time its quantitative nature is enhanced by the very permanence of the coming order.[36]

Colin Brown notes:

> The words life and judgment are what I. T. Ramsey called models which describe something in familiar terms which is, in fact, not capable of being described in a purely literal way. For although eternal life can be entered into now its future character lies hidden beyond this life. The word eternal is what Ramsey termed a *qualifier* which serves as a directive to understand the model in a special way. . . . The qualifier is not simply a literal description of

---

34. Luke 18:30 says the same, but uses a different term for present time.

35. Papaioannou, *Geography of Hell*, 44. His whole discussion in 41–44 is helpful.

36. Papaioannou, *Geography of Hell*, 48.

the noun but a reminder that it is being used in a non-literal sense (cf. such phrases as "heavenly Father," "infinite love"). Similarly the phrase eternal sin (Mk 3:29) does not mean an endless sin but one which has dimensions and ramifications beyond the present life. Eternal judgment is referred to in Heb 6:2 and 2 Thess 1:9. This, like the idea of eternal fire does not necessarily imply that those concerned go on being judged or continue to be consumed. If the metaphor of fire is to be pressed at all, it would imply that the fire of righteousness continues to burn, but that what is consumed once is consumed for good (cf. also Paul's observation about works being consumed by fire, 1 Cor 3:15).[37]

This applies to the eternal sin in Mark 10:30, which does not go on forever but has permanent consequences. It applies to the eternal gospel proclaimed by the angel in Rev 14:6 which is good news relating to the age to come.[38] It applies to the eternal comfort in 2 Thess 2:16, where the comfort is otherworldly but not unending because Paul prays for some more and relates it to the hope in this present life for the world to come.

The phrase "eternal fire" occurs in Matt 18:8; 25:41; and Jude 7. In Jude it was "eternal fire" that destroyed Sodom and Gomorrah, and it is clear from Genesis 19 that the "fire and sulfur" which rained down would have totally consumed anyone living there—just leaving the smoke that Abraham saw from afar (19:28). It was "eternal" in the sense of otherworldly, and the effect but not the process of destruction was unending. In Amos 5:6 and Ezek 20:47–48 the fire of destruction is not quenched, but again the process of destruction does not continue forever.

When it comes to "eternal life" the discussion of qualitative/quantitative meanings is more complex. We noted above that in Matthew, Mark, and Luke, Jesus promises his self-sacrificing followers "eternal life" in the "age to come." But John 17:3 refers to eternal life as a present life knowing God, and one commentator notes:

37. C. Brown, in Brown, *NIDNTT*, 3:99, italics original.
38. See, e.g., Aune, *Revelation*, 826, and Swete, *Revelation*, 282.

The expression "eternal life" (*zōē aiōnios*), corresponding to the basic meaning of *aiōn*, lifetime, as defined by the OT, is to be understood primarily as a life which belongs to God.[39]

If the term is seen as primarily *qualitative*, how far does it always contain *quantitative* elements? If we cannot really imagine what our "spiritual body" promised by Paul will be like, and time is (as philosophers and scientists suggest) a property of space, maybe it would be presumptive to take "time" in the age to come to be a never-ending version of our present time. What does seem clear, however, is that there is a permanence in the age to come that is lacking in our present age, and there must be some quantitative dimension, so

> the life that is of the coming age in quality and yet one which by the very nature of the coming age conveys a certain permanence.[40]

So what about "eternal judgment," "eternal punishment," and "eternal destruction"?

We should first note that the term judgment (*krima*) is a noun ending in *–ma*, which grammarians say means that the result of the act is included.[41] The eternal judgment is judgment relating to the "age to come," and it is the result that is permanent and enduring not the process.

The result of a judgment on a person found guilty is a punishment of some kind. So an "eternal judgment" (Heb 6:2), a judgment relating to the age to come, must result in an "eternal punishment" in that age.

Jesus is the only one to use the actual phrase eternal punishment, and uses it just once:

> And these will go away into eternal punishment, but the righteous into eternal life. (Matt 26:26)

---

39. J. Gurrt, in Brown, *NIDNTT*, 3:832.

40. Papaioannou, *Geography of Hell*, 48.

41. See, e.g., Robertson, *Grammar of the Greek New Testament*, 153.

We will look later at Jesus's teaching, but here the actual "punishment" is not specified. Paul, however, seems to speak of a similar judgment scene to Matt 25 when he predicts for the wicked a day

> when the Lord Jesus is revealed from heaven with his mighty angels in flaming fire, inflicting vengeance on those who do not know God and on those who do not obey the gospel of our Lord Jesus. They will suffer the punishment of eternal destruction. (2 Thess 1:7–9)

Since this is in the age to come the punishment is presumably eternal punishment, and Paul says it is "eternal destruction" in flaming (and presumably eternal) fire. But the consistent biblical teaching is that eternal fire (as in Gen 19:24–29 and Jude 7) implies total destruction, a city or person ceasing to exist as an entity with only a smoke of memory. The actual word here for "destruction" is *olethron*, which means ruin but not necessarily annihilation (as in 1 Cor 5:5 and the unexpected thief in 1 Thess 5:3). However, in its only other NT use, in 1 Tim 6:9, it is linked together with *apōleian*, so the "ruin" can lead to the destruction in the normal sense.

Two more important points can be made about this. Second Thessalonians 1:9 has two grammatically possible renderings:

> These shall be punished with eternal destruction *from the* presence of the Lord and from the glory of His power. (2 Thess 1:9 NKJV)

> They will suffer the punishment of eternal destruction, *away from the* presence of the Lord and from the glory of his might. (2 Thess 1:9 ESV)

The ESV has a footnote that the rendering "from" rather than "away from" is also possible, and the NKJV is joined by, e.g., the ASV, CSB, JUB, WEB, and YLT in this rendering. But which is correct?

Believers in unending torment have claimed that "away from" means that the wicked will suffer permanent "separation from" God, which will leave them permanently in pain and suffering. Is this a plausible rendering of the phrase?

The actual exact Greek phrase (*apo prosōpou tou kyriou*), is used only one other time in Scripture, when Peter pleads with Jews to repent and be forgiven so

> that times of refreshing may come *from the presence of the Lord*, and that he may send the Christ appointed for you, Jesus. (Acts 3:20 ESV)

The times of refreshing are clearly not because they will be *separated from* the presence of the Lord, but will be the *effect of* his presence. The clear implication is that the "presence of the Lord" will bring refreshing to the repentant in Acts but will bring destruction to those in Thessalonians who are persecuting the Christians. It makes no sense to translate the identical phrase differently. In Lev 10:2, "fire came out from the presence of the Lord and consumed them and they died before the Lord," and in Num 16:35, "fire came out from the Lord and consumed the 250 men." The effect is from being in his presence, not from being separated from it; the prophets don't say whether the process was painful but do clearly state it finally results in being consumed by the "flaming fire." The idea of hell as an unending suffering for the wicked because they are separated from God has no basis at all in Scripture.

A second point here is that critics sometimes argue that since "eternal life" means life that lasts forever, so "eternal punishment" and "eternal destruction" must mean processes lasting forever. There are very serious problems with this argument. Eternal life is primarily a quality of life—a life knowing God (John 17:3) that will continue into the age to come. But life is *essentially* a process that *continues*, and to continue permanently presumably implies in some sense unending process. But "destruction" essentially means a termination of something not a continuation, so an eternal punishment of eternal destruction means a termination that is final. In this sense the effect is unending, but the process of judging and destroying is not. Destruction in the present life is not permanent because there will be a resurrection, but in the age to come this effect is permanent.

The eternal judgment of the determinedly unrepentant, the judgment in the age to come, is an eternal punishment that is eternal destruction. This is a destruction that is permanent in effect rather than an unending process.

Hell (Gk: *Gehenna*)

What does the NT term *Gehenna* (usually translated "hell") mean?[42] It is used once allegorically of the tongue in Jas 3:6, and only eleven times elsewhere—all by Jesus.

Some scholars have suggested that the terms *Hades* and *Gehenna* are used interchangeably in the NT, but this is implausible. There is no evidence that any Jewish group believed this at the time of Jesus; moreover, Acts 2:31 speaks of Jesus's *psychē* being not abandoned to Hades, and in Revelation Hades itself is thrown into the lake of fire (and it would be odd if the "Gehenna of fire" were thrown into the lake of fire).

The term *Gehenna* does not appear in Greek literature (or the LXX) but is a form of the Hebrew *Gē Hinnōm*. This was originally a valley south of Jerusalem. Here at one time Moloch had been worshipped in child sacrifice (2 Kgs 23:10; 2 Chr 28:3; 33:6; Jer 7:31; 32:35).

In 7:32 and 19:6 Jeremiah renames it the "valley of slaughter," a judgment on the Jewish apostates:

> And the dead bodies of this people will be food for the birds of the air, and for the beasts of the earth, and none will frighten them away. (Jer 7:33 ESV)

In Isaiah, God promises to make a new heaven and new earth, and adds:

> And they shall go out and look on the dead bodies of the men who have rebelled against me. For their worm shall not die, their fire shall not be quenched, and they shall be an abhorrence to all flesh. (Isa 66:24 ESV)

42. Papaioannou, *Geography of Hell*, 3–81, contains an excellent much longer analysis of this.

Isaiah here does not specify the location, but the similarities to the judgment of the apostate/rebellious in Jeremiah are obvious—whether the dead bodies are consumed by birds and beasts or fire and maggots. Commentators generally associate the two prophecies.

Given that the men are dead, they don't feel anything, and the bodies, presumably, are totally consumed and destroyed. The "worms" do not die before they finish the consumption, and no one will quench the "fire," but the people are not suffering, and the bodies do not last forever. It was "eternal fire" that destroyed Sodom and Gomorrah (Jude 7), and, as already noted, it is clear from Genesis 19 that the "fire and sulfur" which rained down would have totally consumed anyone living there—just leaving the smoke that Abraham saw from afar (19:28). It was "eternal" in the sense of otherworldly, and the effect but not the process of destruction was unending. In Jer 17:27, Amos 5:6, and Ezek 20:47–48 the fire of destruction is not quenched, but again the process of destruction does not continue forever.

Jesus seems to be the first in the first century to refer to the *Gē Hinnōm* location in a context of judgment and eschatology, and Papaioannou shows that Jewish and Christian references to Gehenna are much later.[43] Jesus refers to *Gehenna* in several passages, for example, where the ESV translates it as "hell":

> If your right eye causes you to sin, tear it out and throw it away. For it is better that you lose one of your members than that your whole body be thrown into hell. And if your right hand causes you to sin, cut it off and throw it away. For it is better that you lose one of your members than that your whole body go into hell. (Matt 5:29–30 ESV)

> And do not fear those who kill the body but cannot kill the soul. Rather fear him who can destroy (*apolesai*) both soul and body in hell (Matt 10:28 ESV)

> And if your eye causes you to sin, tear it out and throw it away. It is better for you to enter life with one eye than

43. See, e.g., Papaioannou, *Geography of Hell*, 14–21.

with two eyes to be thrown into the hell of fire. (Matt 18:9 ESV)

If your hand causes you to stumble, cut it off. It is better for you to enter life maimed than with two hands to go into hell, where the fire never goes out. And if your foot causes you to stumble, cut it off. It is better for you to enter life crippled than to have two feet and be thrown into hell. And if your eye causes you to stumble, pluck it out. It is better for you to enter the kingdom of God with one eye than to have two eyes and be thrown into hell, where "the worms that eat them do not die, and the fire is not quenched." (Mark 9:43–48 ESV)

I tell you, my friends, do not fear those who kill the body, and after that have nothing more that they can do. But I will warn you whom to fear: fear him who, after he has killed, has authority to cast into hell. Yes, I tell you, fear him! (Luke 12:4–5 ESV)

In Matt 10:28 (and Luke 12:4–5 is similar) Jesus contrasts how human persecutors can destroy only the body, but God can destroy both body and *psychē* in *Gehenna*. Human tyrants can terminate the body (i.e., take away the life), but not the *psychē* in the sense of that which is the essential life, personality, and personhood of the martyr, which will be resurrected. In the *Gehenna* of fire the destruction is like the all-destroying fire and brimstone that destroyed Sodom, but it is the whole being (body and *psychē*) that can be permanently destroyed.

In both Matthew and Mark, Jesus also notes that to destroy a body part now is preferable to facing the total destruction in *Gehenna*. In Mark, Jesus makes very clear his allusion to Isa 66:24 in the graphic picture of the fire which cannot be quenched and the maggots that will totally consume the bodies in the judgment. But, as we have already seen, in the "destruction" in Isaiah and the instances of OT people being consumed in judgmental fire from God the emphasis is not on prolonged or unending torment but that they cease to exist as entities. The difference here is that it is not just bodies that are destroyed but both the (presumably resurrected) body and *psychē* or essential being cease to exist as entities. And, because it is in the "age to come," the termination is permanent and final.

At the end of a careful analysis, Papaioannou concludes:

> All the Gehenna texts therefore have the following common elements—strong emphasis on the body, judgment after a resurrection, annihilation rather than torment, strong Old Testament influence.[44]

Many other respected commentators have noted these meanings in the references to *Gehenna*. For example Morna Hooker comments on Mark 9:43–48:

> The image seems to be annihilation, in contrast to life; it is the fire, and not the torment, which is unquenchable.[45]

R. T. France comments on these Mark verses that v. 43

> picks up the common imagery of fire as the agent of judgment and destruction, perhaps exploiting the origin of the word Gehenna in the Valley of Hinnom. . . . The wording of this pericope does not in itself settle the question either way, quite apart from the danger of using vivid traditional imagery to establish formal doctrine.[46]

Of Matt 5:22 he notes:

> In this passage it is spoken of as a place of destruction, not of continuing punishment. . . . On the basis of this text alone it would therefore be better to speak of true life (the "soul") not as eternal but as "potentially eternal," since it can be "destroyed" in hell;[47]

It is commonly suggested that the valley of Hinnom later became a garbage dump, though Papaioannou points out that there is insufficient contemporary evidence for this after the time of Josiah. He reiterates, however, that the judgmental allusions in the

---

44. Papaioannou, *Geography of Hell*, 81.

45. Hooker, *Gospel according to Mark*, 232.

46. France, *Gospel of Mark*, 382.

47. France, *Gospel of Matthew*, 403.

OT refer to destruction of bodies, not extended torment, which is the essential point.[48] The ignominious fate of the dead in Isaiah 66:24 in Jesus's allusion itself implies they are treated like rubbish, and the parallel holds without this specific connection. What is involved is destruction, not continued or unending torment.

Eternal Punishment (Gk: *Kolasin Aiōnion*)

The Meaning of *Kolasin/Kolazo*

We have seen how the adjective *aiōnion* is plain enough, meaning that which pertains to the age to come. But what of *kolasin*? In 2 Thess 1:9 the term used for punishment is a different one, which is from *ekdikeō* and means vengeance or punitive justice. So could the use of *kolasin* indicate that the punishment is *not* destruction as Paul and other apostles say but unending torment?

Actually, *kolasin* has no clear unambiguous meaning, and if anything is more general. Thayer's lexicon gives the meaning of the noun *kolasin* as "correction, punishment, penalty" and of the verb *kolazo* as "1. properly, to lop, prune, as trees, wings. 2. to check, curb, restrain. 3. to chastise, correct, punish."[49] Abbot-Smith gives the noun meaning as "correction, penalty, punishment" and the verb meaning as "to curtail, dock, prune. 2. To check, restrain. 3. To chastise, correct, punish."[50] Schneider in the classic *TDNT* links it with its etymology: "to cut short, to lop, to trim, and figuratively a. to impede, restrain, and b. to punish, and in the passive to suffer loss," though his detailed article shows a range of meanings for the term.[51]

There is not a lot of use of either the noun or verb in the Greek LXX.[52] In Ezekiel the noun is used several times to convey

---

48. Papaioannou, *Geography of Hell*, 6.

49. Thayer, *Greek English Lexicon*, 352–53.

50. Abbott-Smith, *Manual Greek Lexicon*, 252.

51. T. Schneider in *TDNT*, iii, 814–17 (300 in the abridged edition).

52. These are listed in Hatch and Redpath, *Concordance*, 2:776; Brown, *NIDNTT*, 3:98; and Schneider in *TDNT*, 3:814–17.

a Hebrew word meaning a cause of stumbling. One version of the LXX has in Dan 6:12(13) Daniel's opponents urging King Darius not to reduce his edict but to "punish" the person who did not abide by it. The "punishment" here was intended to be a gruesome but fairly rapid process culminating in annihilation. The book of the Wisdom of Solomon (11:5, 13) refers to the "punishment" of the Egyptians when they were exterminated in the Red Sea. In a later passage (sometimes mistranslated) it says that the Egyptians were drawn on in spite of their experience of the plagues

> in order that they might fill up the punishment that their torments still lacked. (Wis 19:4 NRSV)

Their punishment (*kolasin*) was completed by their total destruction in the Red Sea.

The Egyptians reappear in Wis 16:1–2 as "punished" by beasts like the "loathsome beasts" (15:18) they worship. In 16:9 they are killed by locusts and flies "because they deserved to be punished by such means." *Kolazo/kolasin* here implies torment that culminates in their deaths.

In the apocryphal books of 1–2 Maccabees the term is occasionally used but is either vague or implies actions leading to death.[53]

In summary, some of the Ezekiel uses of the term imply a "stumbling block," which is surely not Jesus's meaning in Matt 25:46? Some pre-Jesus uses are nonspecific as to its meaning. The others imply a painful process culminating in death/annihilation—ceasing to exist. How then can anyone possibly take it to imply unending torment in the few places it is used in the New Testament?

In the NT the noun *kolasin* is used in Matt 25:46 and in just one other place:

> By this, love is perfected [brought to its higher stages] with us, so that we may continuously have confidence in the day of judgment; because as He is, so also are we in

---

53. The tyrant in 4 Macc 8:9, which postdates Jesus, threatens a "punishment" of torment culminating in complete destruction.

this world. There is no fear in love, but perfect love casts out fear. For fear has to do with punishment, and whoever fears has not been perfected in love. (1 John 4:17–18 ESV)

This seems to be saying that Christians do not need to fear the day of judgment, because we are already in a love relationship with God and will not fear any punishment given on that day. It is not specific what punishment is meant, so does not really help us understand what the punishment might be.

The verb *kolazo* is used twice. In Acts 4:21 the authorities could find no way to *punish* the apostles to stop them preaching; but it does not say what kind of punishment they had in mind. Maybe it was death by stoning, as happened soon after to Stephen, whose case was heard by the same high priest. The other use of the verb is:

> . . . then the Lord knows how to rescue the godly from trials, and to keep the unrighteous under punishment until the day of judgment. (2 Pet 2:9 ESV)

The "punishment" here is a present participle, which most versions (including the ESV) render as a present ongoing action. Bauckham, however, notes that a Greek future passive participle at this time would be rare, and notes that most commentators now see this in terms as he translates it: "*to keep the wicked to be punished at the day of judgment.*"[54] This makes a lot more sense, but unfortunately it does not tell us what the "punishment" at that time will be. Second Peter 3:7, however, tells us explicitly that the day of judgment will bring the *destruction* (*apōleias*) of the ungodly. It would therefore seem odd to think that the earlier verse meant a punishment of unending torment.

There is, in summary, no evidence at all that either the verb *kolazo* or the noun *kolasin* implies prolonged torment.

---

54. Bauckham, *Jude, 2 Peter,* 244, 253–54. This seems more likely than Schneider's view (*TDNT,* 3:816), that it means punishments between death and judgment when their final fate is decided.

The Day of Judgment

In the OT the "day of the Lord" is a day when God will intervene in judgment. Sometimes it refers to more immediate intervention, but some later uses are taken by Christians to refer to the *parousia* of Christ. For these OT references, usually the effect of the wrath and vengeance of God on the day is destruction. In Zeph 1:3 everyone will be destroyed, in Mal 4:5 there will be total destruction, and in Obad 1:15–16 in the day of the Lord the nations opposed to God will be made "as though they had never been." There is no concept of unending torment.

In the NT it is a "day of judgment" (Matt 10:15; 11:22; 11:24; 12:36; 2 Pet 2:9; 3:7; 1 John 4:17) or "day of wrath" (Rom 2:5), and is described in other scenes of judgment (Matt 7:21–23; John 12:48; Acts 17:41; 2 Cor 5:10; 2 Tim 4:8). Paul is quite explicit, as we previously noted, that this will be the time when

> the Lord Jesus is revealed from heaven with his mighty angels in flaming fire, inflicting vengeance on those who do not know God and on those who do not obey the gospel of our Lord Jesus. They will suffer the punishment of eternal destruction. (2 Thess 1:7–9 ESV)

We have noted how this accords with the OT when the presence of the Lord brings fire, and the punishment is destruction. Hebrews 10:27 also refers to "judgment and a fury of fire that will consume the adversarsies." Again, a fire that "consumes" destroys in the sense of obliterates, it does not imply any unending torment. It is a process leading to nonexistence.

Matthew 25:46

All this is background to Jesus's words in Matt 25:46 where he refers to "eternal punishment" (*kolasin aiōnion*).

At the start of Matthew 24 Jesus predicts the destruction of the temple, and his disciples ask:

Tell us, when will these things be, and what will be the
sign of your coming and of the end of the age?

They seem to think this is just one question (after all the fall
of the temple must herald the end of the world!); as R. T. France
points out in his commentary it is actually two. On the second
question Jesus replies that the "coming of the Son of Man" will be a
very public event, but that the timing of "that day" no one knows.
He then continues with various parables (which we will later look
at) to encourage them to stay faithful and ready.

Jesus then begins to speak of

> when the Son of Man comes in his glory, and all the
> angels with him, then he will sit on his glorious throne.
> (Matt 25:31 ESV)

This is obviously reflected in the words just quoted from
2 Thess 1:7–9, and the fury of fire in Heb 10:27—in which the result was total, all-consuming destruction. We should also note that
John the Baptist and Jesus refer to a judgmental fire of God that
totally consumes (Matt 3:10; 3:12; 7:19; 13:40) and in 3:12 it is "unquenchable fire," but obviously the "chaff" will be totally destroyed
and cease to exist as chaff.

In Matt 25 Jesus continues with the famous picture of the
sheep and the goats. There are questions here about whether the
nations assembled include everyone or just those purporting to be
Christians and calling him "Lord," and whether the "least of these
my brothers" means Christians or anyone. In any event, Jesus's
main purpose here (consistent with Matt 16:27) is surely to encourage his followers to show the spontaneous acts of compassion
which we know flow out from being in fellowship with God, on
which point John also expands in his letters. But the emphasis on
lifestyle leads the conservative evangelical scholar R. T. France, in
his great commentary, to go as far as to say:

> So it does not seem possible to read this passage as ex-
> pressing a "Pauline" salvation of explicit faith in Jesus.[55]

---

55. France, *Gospel of Matthew*, 959.

The picture is not to supplant faith with works of the law, nor to give some new or novel perception on the fate of those who don't do such acts, but to encourage followers to live out the faith-life. The alternative is *eternal punishment*, but it would be very odd to ascribe to this single phrase, using a word for punishment which can take a range of meanings, a view of the final judgment of the unrepentant which departs both from his own terms of "destruction" and being totally consumed, and from all the other references in all the other NT writers. But to take *kolasin aiōnion* to mean unending torment without hope would be to do exactly this.

Various renowned conservative scholars have noted this. R. T. France says on this Matthew 25 passage:

> In the debate among evangelical theologians on the issue of annihilation as against continuing punishment, the phrase "eternal punishment" here in Matt 25:46 is commonly cited as a proof-text for the latter position. But this is usually on the assumption that "eternal" is a synonym for "everlasting." That assumption depends more on modern English usage than on the meaning of *aiōnios*, which we have seen to be related to the concept of the two ages. "Eternal punishment," so understood, is punishment which relates to the age to come rather than punishment which continues forever, so that the term does not in itself favour one side or the other in the annihilationist debate. Insofar as the metaphor of fire may be pressed, however, it suggests destruction rather than punishment. . . . The imagery of incineration in relation to the final destiny of the wicked also occurs more explicitly in 13:42; the weeds are destroyed, not kept burning forever. We have noted the use of the verb "destroy" in relation to hell in 10:28. These points suggest that the annihilationist theology (sometimes described as "conditional immortality") does more justice to Matthew's language in general, and if so the sense of "eternal punishment" here will not be "punishment which goes on forever" but "punishment which has eternal

consequences," the loss of eternal life through being destroyed by fire.[56]

Colin Brown's section on the phrase *kolasin aiōnion* in the *NIDNTT* has already been quoted in the section on "eternal," and on Matt 25:46 he specifically says:

> The passage has often been cited in support of the doctrine of endless torment. But it may be questioned whether it implies more than the finality of judgment. The term eternal has both qualitative and quantitative overtones. . . . Jesus did not teach like Plato and others that the soul was intrinsically immortal and that it would necessarily go on after death.[57]

Should we believe that in the age to come there will be an eternal judgment leading to an eternal punishment? Yes indeed: that eternal punishment will be eternal destruction, a destruction of body and *psychē* that (whatever the process is) is final. But it does not lead to unending torment without hope. There is no reference to torment in Matthew 25.

As noted in the final chapter below, this seems to be how the early church theologian Irenaeus saw eternal punishment: the effects not the process are unending.

---

56. France, *Gospel of Matthew*, 966.

57. C. Brown, in Brown, *NIDNTT*, 3:99.

3

The Jewish Background

We have looked already at various OT references, and in general the fate of the wicked is portrayed as "destruction." The smoke of this may ascend indefinitely (or for a long time) as a memorial, but there is nowhere any concept of a fate of unending suffering without hope.

Advocates of the "traditional" unending torment hell sometimes cite ideas contained in non-biblical Jewish works written before or during the first century. The suggestion is that a belief in unending torment was common among Jewish contemporaries of Jesus, so it would be natural to take his references to *Gehenna* and eternal punishment as implying this. This suggestion seems to be mistaken.

Pre-Jesus Sources

Judith

This may have been written around 100 BCE, and is accepted by Catholics and Orthodox Churches as Scripture, but not by Protestants or Jews. Its history is muddled, and its geographical descriptions unidentifiable, but it is a rattling good story about a beautiful

Jewish heroine who cleverly assassinates an invading general. At the end of her song of triumph she says:

> Woe to the nations that rise up against my people! The Lord Almighty will take vengeance on them in the day of judgment; he will send fire and worms into their flesh; they shall weep in pain for ever. (Jdt 16:17 NRSV)

It is to be doubted that one sentence in the triumph over a tyrant song of a probably fictional character in a book later rejected by the Jews as Scripture indicates any general Jewish view of the fate of unbelievers. But in any case is the translation made of her phrase a good one? On this latter point, the key final phrase is *heōs aiōnos* Here *heōs* means "until" and *aiōnos* is the genitive form of *aiōn* which means "an age." So in the LXX of 1 Chr 15:2 the Levites were said to have been chosen to minister *heōs aiōnos*. In Jer 7:7 the Jews were promised that if they acted justly they could possess the land *heōs aiōnos*. A fairly similar phrase is used in Matt 28:20, *heōs tes synteleias tou aiōnos*, which is generally translated "unto the end of the age." So it is doubtful that even "Judith" believed in unending torture, let alone that it was a general belief.

1 Enoch

As the biblical book of Revelation is apocalyptic, earlier or contemporary apocalyptic material could be relevant to our understanding.

In the *NIDNTT*, H. C. Hahn states:

> In Jewish apocalyptic of the intertestamental and NT period, the idea appears of an eschatological destruction of the world, sometimes conceived in terms of a world conflagration. The ungodly will perish along with the world.[1]

In other words, this follows the OT idea that the wicked will be destroyed, not suffer for unending time without hope.

---

1. H. C. Hahn, in Brown, *NIDNTT*, 1:463.

The voluminous commentaries on 1 Enoch cannot be summarized here, but our particular concern is: does it imply unending torment after the last judgment on the unrighteous? Right throughout its sections there is reference to the great day of judgment or day of destruction (1:9; 10:6; 16:2; 19:2; 22:4; 22:11; 45:6; 62:8; 81:4; 84:4; 94:9; 97:3; 98:10; 99:15; 100:4; 102:5; 104:5). So our concerns may be what happens to dead humans awaiting that day, and what happens afterward.

The earliest part 11–36 relates how the fallen angels (watchers) will be judged by the "Lord of Spirits." The watchers and their leader Azazel are immortal as against mortal humans (10:8) and carry most blame for human sin (10:8). After various imprisonments "for ever and ever" Azazel will be "cast into the fire" (10:6). In the day of great judgment (10:12). Elledge notes how

> later portions of the book develop a more complex anthropology to describe how immortal watchers became susceptible to destruction (15:4–6). . . . All other human evildoers will share their fate of cosmic imprisonment and everlasting destruction in the infernal realms (10:14).[2]

Throughout 1 Enoch, the final fate of the sinful and oppressors is perish or be destroyed (1:9; 10:16; 10:22; 42:2; 45:10; 53:2; 53:5; 69:27; 92:11; 96:8; 97:2; 98:3; 99:9; 99:16). When the "spirits" of deceased sinners are cast into the "furnace of fire" they will perish (98:3). Earlier it graphically says of this:

> *As straw in the fire and as lead in the water, thus they will burn before the face of the holy,* and they will sink before the face of the righteous, and *no trace of them will be found.* (48:9)

Others will have opportunity to repent, but "he who repents not before him shall perish."

Aune says many commentators have pointed out that in 1 Enoch the wicked "will be forever judged and tormented before

---

2. Elledge, *Resurrection of the Dead*, 133.

the righteous,"[3] but this is misleading. Of the punishment of the wicked it says:

> And they will be a spectacle for the righteous and for
> his chosen ones; and: they will rejoice over them . . .
> the righteous and the chosen will be saved on that day,
> and the face of the sinners and the unrighteous they will
> henceforth not see. (62:12–13).

But the "spectacle" cannot last interminably because the righteous see their faces no more, and the "elect one" will slay all the sinners by the word of his mouth (62:2).

Whatever we make of the somewhat ambiguous end-prophesies of the immortal fallen angels, there is no basis in 1 Enoch to suggest that unending torment will be the final end for unrepentant humans.

Dead Sea Scrolls

The Dead Sea Scrolls repeatedly promise "everlasting destruction" or "utter destruction" to the wicked, meaning "they shall have no remnant or survivor." So, e.g., they promise the wicked a visitation of plagues and

> everlasting damnation by the avenging wrath of the fury
> of God, eternal torment and endless disgrace together
> with shameful extinction in the fire of the dark regions.
> The times of all their generations shall be spent in sor-
> rowful mourning and in bitter misery and in calamities
> of darkness until they are destroyed without remnant or
> survivor.[4]

Where there is torment in the age to come it leads to cessation of existence; the disgrace is endless because there is shame in the extinction. Without this context, the use of the phrase "eternal torment" by modern Christians is misleading.

---

3. Aune, *Revelation 6–16*, 835.
4. Vermes, *Dead Sea Scrolls*, 134 and 149 (locations 2111, 2328).

Elledge looks through the various Dead Sea sources, for example in Pseudo-Ezekiel. He notes, however, in the 4Qinstruction:

> And all those who will endure forever, those who seek the truth, shall awaken to judge y[ou. And then] will all the foolish minded be destroyed, and the children of iniquity shall not be found anymore, [and a]ll those who hold fast to wickedness shall wither [away]. (4Q418 frg. 69 II 4–8)[5]

There seems no indication in the Dead Sea Scrolls for anything other than destruction as the eventual fate of the wicked.

Powys notes the divergences among early rabbinical schools, and that

> it is thus not certain that *"Gehenna"* when employed in the early Rabbinic literature consistently or ordinarily denoted unending suffering.[6]

Papaioannou notes that *Gē Hinnōm* was not associated with the punishment of the wicked in any records between Jeremiah and Jesus's teaching; he says that "the earliest Jewish references cannot be dated earlier than AD 70," and that "the New Testament material represents an earlier stage than extrabiblical Jewish writings in the development of the *Gehenna* tradition."[7]

The much later Jewish Talmud contains a number of divergent ideas, some holding that the wicked go straight to Gehenna, and are not resurrected for judgment as the New Testament teaches everyone will be.

Apart from the fact that their views on what constituted righteousness differed significantly from Jesus and the apostles, such sources can offer little to help us understand Jesus's use of *Gehenna*.

---

5. Elledge, *Resurrection of the Dead*, 170.

6. Powys, *"Hell,"* 190.

7. Papaioannou, *Geography of Hell*, 24–25.

Psalms of Solomon & 2 Maccabees

We noted in looking at the ideas of resurrection that in pre-Jesus sources the fate of the wicked was simply to not get resurrected at all, they permanently ceased to exist. In the Psalms of Solomon (second or first century BCE) the destruction of the sinner is forever, but "they that fear the Lord shall rise to life eternal" (3:16). In the second-century BCE book of 2 Maccabees,[8] the heroes look forward to resurrection to life but warn the tyrant that there will be no such resurrection for him (7:9). Typical are the words of son number four:

> One cannot but choose to die at the hands of mortals, and to cherish the hope that God gives of being raised by him. But for you there will be no resurrection to life! (2 Macc 7:14 NRSV)

The sixth son says:

> Do not think that you will go unpunished[9] for having tried to fight against God. (2 Macc 7:19 NRSV)

There is no assumption here of human immortality. There is nothing about unending suffering. While there will be judgment for the ungodly, the resurrection to life is promised only to the faithful. For those who "fall asleep in godliness" there is an expectation that they will rise again (12:44).

Post-Jesus Teaching

There was a change during the first two centuries as the older Jewish and Christian ideas about Hades and human mortality were affected by Hellenistic ideas.[10] Various post-Jesus Jewish sources evidence this increasing Hellenistic influence. We looked briefly at some of these in the above section on the soul.

8. Some scholars put the final redaction later than the second century.

9. The word used is *athóos*, meaning unpunished or innocent.

10. Bauckham, *Fate of the Dead*, 34. There is a story of reversed fortunes in the Palestinian Talmud (y. Sank. 23c; y. Hag. 77d) which is written much later.

Philo of Alexandria

Philo gives no clear discussion of his view of human immortality in general, and the only thing which seems clear is his belief that the virtuous souls will survive death and be reborn into some incorporeal existence. There is no description of heaven or hell.

Four Maccabees

The book we call 4 Maccabees is not accepted as Scripture by anyone (Jews, Protestants, Catholics or Orthodox Christians). It was written in elegant Greek by a diaspora Jew and its date is disputed and uncertain, but seemingly post-Jesus.[11] It retells the much earlier 2 Maccabees account of the martyrdom of seven Jewish brothers, but its slant is a kind of Greek Neoplatonic/Stoic idea that reason rules over passion. In it, all the seven brothers give a long speech in unison, ending, "You, because of your bloodthirstiness toward us, will deservedly undergo from the divine justice eternal torment by fire" (9:9). None of this is in the earlier 2 Maccabees. Later, the long speech of the youngest brother in 2 Maccabees is altered to promise the tyrant "eternal fire and tortures, and these throughout all time will never let you go" (4 Macc 12:12). The resurrection of the body (accepted by 2 Maccabees, by the Pharisees, and by Paul) is not stated in 4 Maccabees, but rather all human souls seem immortal, as assumed in some Greek philosophy. David DeSilva describes in detail how the Jewish adherence to Torah is presented in a Greco-Roman fashion as exhibiting virtues of reason, courage, and wisdom, which were valued.[12] This was to encourage diaspora Jews to hold on to Jewish laws in face of persecution. Its relationship with Josephus and Philo is interesting but beyond our present scope.[13]

---

11. DeSilva, *Four Maccabees*, n113, implies either about 40 CE or 100 CE.

12. Desilva, *Four Maccabees*, chapters 1 and 2.

13. The relationship of Philo and 4 Maccabees is discussed in Cornthwaite, "Torah in the Diaspora."

The story of the martyrs had resonance in the church under persecution (though Origen cites 2 Macc not 4 Macc). Fourth Maccabees' theological deviances from the teachings of Jesus and Paul are also fairly obvious, even if there are points of contact through a common Jewish heritage. But the real question is whether its particular view of divine post-death torture of tyrants represents (say) Plato or the views of Jesus's Jewish contemporaries in Judaea. Given the pre-Jesus works in 2 Maccabees, the Dead Sea scrolls, and even 1 Enoch, it seems unlikely that they do.

Wisdom of Solomon

In this probably first-century Alexandrian-influenced work the righteous have a hope of resurrection but there is no indication of an unending torment fate for the unrighteous.

Josephus

Josephus wrote his *Wars* (ca. 75 CE) and *Antiquities* (ca. 94 CE). In *Wars* 2:8 he refers to the three groups: Pharisees, Sadducees and Essenes, and in *Antiquities* adds that the Pharisees:

> Believe that souls have an immortal vigour in them: and that under the earth there will be rewards, or punishments; according as they have lived virtuously or viciously in this life: and the latter are to be detained in an everlasting prison; but that the former shall have power to revive and live again.(*Ant* 18:14)

Paul, much earlier, had indicated that Pharisees like himself believed in the bodily resurrection of both just and unjust, but Josephus wanted to ingratiate himself with his benefactors, and Greco-Romans rejected bodily resurrection, so this is not mentioned.

The Essenes he describes sound in lifestyles much like the Dead Sea group, but in *Wars* 2:8:11 he ascribes to them a belief that immortal souls are entangled in bodies, and when released from this "slavery" are carried upward. He claims they held a view very like the Greeks, that the good are carried off into a pleasant place and the bad into a murky and stormy recess, filled with unceasing retributions. This resembles 1 Enoch, but one may wonder how much is given from a desire to please Greco-Roman thinking. It does not seem evidenced in the Dead Sea Scrolls if these were connected with his Essenes.

Josephus does not mention Gehenna or unending torment. The *Discourse on Hades* once ascribed to him is a fake, written by Bishop Hippolytus a century later.

Later Thinking

Post first-century Jewish thinking developed, and various opinions are given in the Mishnah and Talmud. Christian thinking also developed, confusing Hades and Gehenna and offering tours of heaven and hell like the earliest one, the second-century *Apocalypse of Peter*. They do not indicate Jewish beliefs at the time of Jesus, and diverge from the view of a general resurrection described by Jesus and his apostles. Likewise, works like 4 Ezra and 2 Baruch have Hellenistic views of the afterlife, but again do not indicate such were common among Jesus's Jewish contemporaries.

4

New Testament Teaching

Judgment

However we understand the details, it is clear that there will be a day of judgment, and *everyone* in Sheol will be raised and judged:

> . . . just as people are destined to die once, and after that to face judgment. (Heb 9:27 NET)

> . . . on the day of wrath when God's righteous judgment will be revealed. He will render to each one according to his works: to those who by patience in well-doing seek for glory and honor and immortality, he will give eternal life; but for those who are self-seeking and do not obey the truth, but obey unrighteousness, there will be wrath and fury. (Rom 2:5–8 ESV)

> Do not marvel at this, for an hour is coming when all who are in the tombs will hear his voice and come out, those who have done good to the resurrection of life, and those who have done evil to the resurrection of judgment. (John 5:28–29 ESV)

> For we must all appear before the judgment seat of Christ, so that each one may receive what is due for what he has done in the body, whether good or evil. Therefore, knowing the fear of the Lord, we persuade others. (2 Cor 5:10–11 ESV)

> And the dead were judged according to their works, as recorded in the books. And the sea gave up the dead that were in it, Death and Hades gave up the dead that were in them, and all were judged according to what they had done. (Rev 20:12–13 NRSV)

Judgment is at the time of general resurrection, and based on lifestyle. The "what he had done" does not mean clocking up "good works," but living a life in harmony with God, receiving undeserved forgiveness through the blood of Christ, and living out that relationship in righteous lifestyle (see 1 John 3:7). Christians will also face the judgment, but

> love has been perfected among us in this: that we may have boldness on the day of judgment, because as he is, so are we in this world. There is no fear in love, but perfect love casts out fear; for fear has to do with punishment, and whoever fears has not reached perfection in love. (1 John 4:17–18 NRSV)

For the unrepentant there will be degrees of suffering on the day of judgment depending on the amount of guilt:

> They will receive the greater condemnation. (Mark 12:40 ESV)

> But I tell you that it will be more tolerable on the day of judgment for the land of Sodom than for you. (Matt 11:24 ESV)

The day of judgment for the unrepentant will involve fear and suffering in varying degrees. But this is on "the Day"; what is the *ultimate* fate of these people? The New Testament says consistently that it will be *destruction*.

Statements of Destruction

We have noted that in Greek the focus of the noun judgment (*krima*) is the result, so for the "eternal judgment" the "eternal punishment" is (as Paul said in 2 Thess 1:9) "eternal destruction." It is destruction which is permanent.

We have also seen that throughout Scripture judicial destruction (whether human or from divine fire) means that a city or individual ceases to exist as an entity. This is not based on any obscure argument or complicated grammatical point, and it is not put in doubt when very occasionally the term is used differently in a metaphorical non-judgment context.

Some church groups include in their statement of faith a belief in "unending torment" or "eternal torment." Notably, neither phrase appears anywhere in Scripture. For human suffering of pain, the term *basanos* is used once in Luke 16:23 but this refers only to Hades awaiting resurrection, not to the final punishment.[1] There is no use of the term to imply judgmental pain in Matthew, Mark, John, the Acts, the letters of Paul, Hebrews, the letters of Peter, the letters of John, or the letter of Jude. What all these biblical books tell us is that the final end of the determinedly unrepentant is *destruction*. So let us look at what is consistently said about the final judgment on the unrepentant being destruction:

> 1. Matt 7:13: "Enter by the narrow gate. For the gate is wide and the way is easy that leads to *destruction* (*apōleian*), and those who enter by it are many." (ESV)

No mention here of unending suffering without hope.

> 2. Matt 10:28: "And do not fear those who kill the body but cannot kill the soul. Rather fear him who can *destroy* (*apolesai*) both soul and body in hell." (ESV)

No mention here of unending suffering without hope.

---

1. And we have also seen that it is far from clear that Jesus meant this to teach us what Hades would actually be like.

3. John 3:16: "For God so loved the world, that he gave his only Son, that whoever believes in him should not perish (*apolētai*) but have eternal life." (ESV)

No mention here of unending suffering without hope.[2]

4. Phil 3:19: "Their end is *destruction* (*apōleia*); their god is the belly; and their glory is in their shame; their minds are set on earthly things." (ESV)

No mention here of unending suffering without hope

5. 1 Tim 6:9: "But those who desire to be rich fall into temptation, into a snare, into many senseless and harmful desires that plunge people into ruin and *destruction* (*apōleian*)." (ESV)

No mention here of unending suffering without hope

6. Heb 10:39: "But we are not of those who shrink back and are *destroyed* (*apōleian*), but of those who have faith and preserve their souls." (ESV)

No mention here of unending suffering without hope

7. Jas 4:12: "There is only one lawgiver and judge, the one who is able to save and *destroy* (*apolesai*). But who are you to judge your neighbor?" (ESV)

No mention here of unending suffering without hope

8. 2 Pet 3:7: "By the same word the present heavens and earth are reserved for fire, being kept for the day of judgment and *destruction* (*apōleias*) of the ungodly." (ESV)

No mention here of unending suffering without hope

In each of these NT verses, if the fate of unbelievers really were unending suffering or torment without hope, surely the

---

2. The version of this in many "Reformed" theologies, sadly, would be: "For God so loved the elect that he sent his only Son, that whoever was sovereignly individually predestined to have faith in him should not suffer unending torment without hope but have unending life." It is hard to see how this could be called "Good News."

writers would have clearly stated it? Surely the writers would not have expected us to take an interpretation of *apollymi* which is never its meaning when referring to punitive judgmental action on an individual or nation? Virtually all modern translations render the term as "destroy" or "destruction." The ancient English term "perdition" originally meant utter destruction, and only because the term is unfamiliar do some people take it to mean a state of unending torment. If the NT writers meant something else than total destruction, then surely they would have said this or explained it?

So if the consistent plain teaching of all these New Testament writers is that the ultimate fate of the unrepentant is destruction, on what kind of scriptural bases have theologians ignored this or taken the term in a strange sense, to proclaim a doctrine of unending suffering without hope?

There are four main biblical elements to which they refer. First, there is Jesus's reference to hellfire—and we have seen he actually says this involves total destruction. Secondly, there is Jesus's single reference to "eternal punishment"—and irreversible extinction *is* an eternal punishment. Thirdly, there are various parables Jesus told—at which we will look next. And finally there is torment in the book of Revelation—at which we will look later.

Parables & Outer Darkness

Some earlier scholars (e.g., Joachim Jeremias) suggested that each parable had just one point. Craig Blomberg has argued that parables can have one point, two points, or three allegorical points.[3] But we should still ask: At whom is it aimed? And what is/are its main point(s)? Pressing a parable beyond this can be risky.

We have looked at the parables of the sheep and the goats, and the rich man and Lazarus. In a number of other parables Jesus talks about splitting people into two groups at the *parousia* or final judgment. The following cover the various types of reference:

1. The wheat and the weeds in the world: Matt 13:24–30, 36–43.

3. Blomberg, *Interpreting the Parables*.

2. The vineyard tenants: Luke 20:1–20.

3. The feast in the kingdom of heaven: Matt 8:11–12.

4. The wedding feast: Matt 22:1–14.

5. The wise and foolish servants: Matt 24:45–51.

6. The ten virgins at the wedding: Matt 25:1–13.

7. The servants with talents: Matt 25:13–30.

In some of these parables there is mention of "weeping and gnashing of teeth." In the OT, the "gnashing of teeth" indicates not pain but anger,[4] and weeping in the Bible generally indicates regret and sorrow. Neither seems to be a reaction to actual pain. In all these parables, then, what is involved is anger and regret at "missing out." But do these parables indicate a fate for unbelievers of being in torment forever?

In (1) the Matt 13 parable of the wheat and weeds is unlike most in that it is a general indication of the final judgment separation into "evil and righteous." The evil will be thrown into a "fiery furnace," like weeds being destroyed in a fire after a harvest. John the Baptist also spoke of the wheat being gathered but the chaff being burned with unquenchable fire (Matt 3:12; Luke 3:17). The fire is unquenchable, but the chaff is obliterated by it. The implication in Matt 13 is that the unrepentant may have regret and anger (teeth gnashing and weeping) but will be consumed, burned, and no longer exist.

In parables (2)–(4) the parables are aimed at those Jews who relied on their descent or ritual observance as assurance of being part of the people of God.

So in (2) the vineyard tenants parable is clearly a warning to the Jewish chief priests and lawyers to be faithful to God and accept him as Messiah. Instead, they kill the son in the parable, and so the enraged father comes to "destroy" them. Does this mean the obliteration of their Jewish temple system coming in 70 CE, or

---

4. T. McComisky, in Brown, *NIDNTT*, 2:421. See also Fudge, *Fire That Consumes*, 158.

does it mean at the final judgment? Possibly both, but the indication is not torment but destruction/obliteration.

In parable (3) the patriarchs sit at the kingdom table with some gentiles, while some of the Jews who relied on their descent are placed outside in the place that they would have placed the gentiles, and they will have regret and anger at missing out on the kingdom celebrations. They are thrown into "outer darkness," but what does this mean? Is it the same as the lake of fire in Revelation? We noted above that in 1 Enoch 10:5 Azazel will be bound and placed in darkness "for ever," but this apparently means to the end of the age because then "in the great day of judgment let him be cast into the fire" (1 Enoch 10:6). Jude 6 likewise speaks of the fallen angels being bound in "eternal chains," but this is only until the "judgment of the great day." Later, Jude 13 compares the false teachers to "wandering stars for whom the gloom of utter darkness has been reserved forever." Bauckham explains the metaphorical background, and,

> unlike the true Christian teachers who are to shine like the stars in heaven (Dan 12:3), the misleading light of the false teachers will be extinguished in darkness forever . . . extinguished in the eternal blackness of the underworld.[5]

So outer darkness is not the same as the lake of fire, and the only other indication we have is either extinction or that it is temporary not permanent. There is no indication of any human torment there. Sometimes people claim that "outer darkness" means "separation from God," and so is "torment." But God is everywhere (Ps 139:7–12), and the idea that "separation from God" (even were this possible) produces torment for sinners is also implausible. In Rev 6:16 the wicked are desperate to *hide* from the face of God, any torment will be from being in his presence not from being separated from it. We noted above that some take 2 Thess 1:9 to imply that the unrighteous suffer from being "separated from" God; but the use of the identical phrase in Acts 3:20 implies that in his presence the righteous are refreshed and the unrepentant destroyed.

5. Bauckham, *Jude, 2 Peter*, 92.

The Matt 22 wedding feast, parable (4), is again primarily a shot at the unfaithful Jewish leaders. Verse 7 says: "The king was angry, and he sent his troops and destroyed those murderers and burned their city." This hints that it was not only indifference but murder of which they were guilty, and the result would be their city being burned and they themselves "destroyed." Was this in 70 CE or at the final judgment? Again probably both, but there is no mention of torment here. The odd twist to the parable is the part about the guest inappropriately dressed. Augustine suggested that the king himself provided garments, but R. T. France notes that there is no evidence of this, and the fault was that the man had not gone home to put on a decent clean white robe:

> The symbolism is of someone who presumes on the free offer of salvation by assuming that therefore there are no obligations attached, someone whose life belies their profession: faith without works. Entry to the kingdom of heaven may be free, but to continue in it carries conditions.[6]

But some things here may be puzzling. If, in the timescale, the feast is post resurrection and judgment, how can he be discovered to have got in only at this point? Were the heavenly bouncers not looking? Is his exclusion permanent? Jesus does not say. Is he to be kept in time-without-end misery while those who more directly rebelled are annihilated? This seems unlikely. Anyway, maybe this is why Peter later tells us to make *our* calling and election (chosenness) sure (2 Pet 1:10). There is no mention of torment, and the same questions are here as already noted about the "outer darkness." All this shows the dangers of trying to press the words in Jesus's parable beyond his central points—unfaithful Israel will be judged and those who think they are part of the people of God better make sure they really are.

We then come to three parables in Matt 24–25. The discourse begins in 24:3 when the disciples ask two questions (though they may think it is only one): "When will these things be, and what will

---

6. France, *Gospel of Matthew*, 826. Endorsed in Blomberg, *Parables*, 311.

be the sign of your coming and the end of the age?" R. T. France shows in his detailed study that in Matt 24:4–35 Jesus is speaking of the events surrounding the destruction of Jerusalem, and from 24:36 Jesus turns to the *parousia*, the second coming. But Jesus does not answer their question as to the *sign* of his *parousia*, because he wants to emphasize that it will be unexpected.[7] His fundamental point is verse 42: "Therefore keep watch, because you don't know the day when your Lord will come." So parables (5), (6), and (7) are not to teach about the nature of the afterlife, but to warn his followers to stay faithful and live right, because no one knows when Jesus will return (although surprisingly there are those today who think they can work it out from biblical prophecy or signs). There is no reason to suppose here that the servants were not really servants, or the foolish virgins not expected for the wedding procession.

In parable (5) the servant can choose either to behave well or to behave badly. If he chooses badly then he will be "cut in two pieces and assigned a place with the hypocrites where there will be weeping and gnashing of teeth." If you cut someone in two pieces they die and cannot show regret and anger. Luke in his parallel 12:42–48 adds that unfaithful servants will receive different numbers of lashes; but if the "lashing" went on for unending time then actually all would get the same number—infinity. Parables are just not to be taken like this; Jesus is making a dramatic point about dire consequences if Christians lapse, not telling us about the nature of the afterlife as such.

The ten virgins (or maidens) in parable (6) do not relate to any known Jewish custom, but were presumably to carry torches (not lamps) in a special show arranged by or for the groom. Being unprepared they missed the procession, and were told they couldn't join the feast. They were not sent for torture, not in torment, nor necessarily left in the dark (they now had oil for torches), but just missed out on the celebration.

Parable (7), the final parable, is again a warning to his disciples. The talents (huge sums of money) are presumably the gifts

---

7. France, *Gospel of Matthew*, 896–943.

given by God to Christians, and we are expected to use them pro-
ductively. The Christian who does not do this is cast out, and has
anger and regret—but is not tormented by torturers forever. In
John 15:6, after Judas has left, Jesus warns them that if they do not
abide in him then they will be cut off, burned, and destroyed, like
an unproductive branch. But there is nothing in any of this about
unending torment.

So in these parables is Jesus intending Christians just to take
the fundamental point of keeping faithful watch, rather than trying to guess exactly what kind of fate awaits those who don't? Are
these maybe parallel to a Christian in 1 Cor 3:15 who builds badly
and will be saved as through fire but "suffer loss," and so in some
sense may weep with regret and gnash teeth with anger?

In summary, none of these parables is aiming to present a
consistent picture of the afterlife, and certainly none of them men-
tions unending torment. If any such idea is read into them it must
be obtained from elsewhere. Generally, the only remotely plausible
source of this idea is the book of Revelation, which we may now
consider.

The Book of Revelation

Perhaps the most common basis on which Christians deny the NT
teaching on destruction is indeed the words in Revelation, in particular Rev 14:9–11 and 20:14. These are taken to mean unending
torment, without hope, in the lake of fire, not only for Satan but
for all human unbelievers. We need, then, to look very carefully at
how to interpret these passages.

Cultural Context and Genre

We will not be concerned here with the structure or provenance
of Revelation, or its place in the Johannine literature,[8] but we are

---

8. For which see, e.g., Bauckham, *Theology of the Book of Revelation*, and
Witherington, *Revelation*.

concerned with its genre. The relevant section of Revelation is a prophetic apocalyptic work which has special characteristics.

The book of Daniel is one obvious precursor. It contains, however, little about the judgment fate of the wicked, other than in Dan 12:2 to say that many of the dead will arise to eternal life or eternal shame. There is no mention of torment.

The apocryphal book of 1 Enoch has some similar imagery, but we have noted that in general the fate of the wicked is seen as destruction, meaning that they cease to exist, albeit after some suffering during the judgment process.

G. K. Beale well expounds why the self-introduction in Revelation indicates that it is primarily symbolic, and not literal. Thus, e.g., the hail and fire in Rev are not predictions of future literal fire and hail but are "clearly figurative."[9]

Analytical commentators on Revelation all tend to warn about the difficulties of interpreting it. Beale explains how

> some comparative figures of speech are intended as visual pictures needing interpretation, while others are meant only to be perceived on a more abstract mental level.[10]

He goes on to say that we should not try to "harmonize" the multiple pictures, but

> the purpose of the combination is to "overwhelm the imagination" and to express ideas that together transcend pictorial visualization.[11]

Bruce Metzger says of Revelation:

> This book contains a series of word pictures, as though a number of slides were being shown on a great screen. As we watch we allow ourselves to be carried along by the impressions created by these pictures. Many of the details of the pictures are intended to contribute to the

9. Beale, *Book of Revelation*, 55.

10. Beale, *Book of Revelation*, 57.

11. Beale, *Book of Revelation*, 57, citing Caird, *Language and Imagery of the Bible*, 149.

overall impression, and are not to be isolated and interpreted with wooden literalism.[12]

Robert Mounce points out:

Informed sensitivity to the thought forms and vocabulary of apocalyptic is the *sine qua non* of satisfactory exegesis.[13]

Richard Bauckham notes:

Revelation does not predict a series of events as though it were history written in advance. Such a misunderstanding of the book cannot survive a sensitive and serious study of its imagery.[14]

Great care needs to be taken in any dogmatic interpretation of the picture imagery in the book of Revelation.

A further issue is whether the images refer to past, present, future, or all of them. Commentators have differed on this:

1. The *Preterist* interpretations see the images as most or all filled by events concerned with first-century Rome (presented as "Babylon").

2. The *Historicist* interpretations of Revelation see the entities and images as corresponding to particular figures throughout church history.

3. The *Futuristic* views picture the images as prophetic accounts of the future.

4. The *Idealist* view sees the images not as referring to specific individuals or events, but as symbols of similar entities throughout history.

A primarily *Idealist* view tends to be taken by most modern commentators. In this view, for example, the beast from the sea is

---

12. Metzger, *Breaking the Code*, 16.

13. Mounce, *Book of Revelation*, 12.

14. Bauckham, *Theology of the Book of Revelation*, 150. This short book gives a brilliant analysis of the genre and nature of Revelation.

interpreted as any state or any human kingdom that is in opposition to God. This would include the Roman Empire (and some aspects do closely relate to Nero) but would broadly apply to all similar empires. Scholars take their cue from the parallels between Rev 13 and Dan 7, noting that in Dan 7:17 the beasts are revealed as kingdoms. This *Idealist* view can be combined with other elements, so Beale also sees the symbols as partly historical or future prophetic. He says:

> The view of this commentary: Eclecticism or a Redemptive-Historical Form of Modified Idealism.[15]

This, he says, fits with past commentators such as Caird, Johnson, and Swete.

Death and Hades

Revelation contains a lot of complex imagery, and sometimes refers to it paradoxically. Thus, for example, regarding Death and Hades (which are often linked):

> Fear not, I am the first and the last, and the living one. I died, and behold I am alive forevermore, and I have the keys of Death and Hades. (Rev 1:17–18 ESV)

> And I looked, and behold, a pale horse! And its rider's name was Death, and Hades followed him. (Rev 6:8 ESV)

> And the sea gave up the dead who were in it, Death and Hades gave up the dead who were in them, and they were judged, each one of them, according to what they had done. Then Death and Hades were thrown into the lake of fire. This is the second death, the lake of fire. And if anyone's name was not found written in the book of life, he was thrown into the lake of fire. (Rev 20:13–15 ESV)

In the first and third of these, Death and Hades are places to which someone can have keys, and from which let people out. In

---

15. Beale, *Book of Revelation*, 48. Bauckham sees much immediate Roman Empire reference, but it is also general principle.

the second one Death is apparently riding a horse, while in the last both Death and Hades are thrown into the lake of fire which is the second death. Aune describes the complex imagery of Death and Hades as personified in the OT, Jewish and Greek thinking (so, e.g., "Hades" in Greek thinking could be a place or a deity).[16] Paul likewise personifies death:

> Yet death reigned from Adam to Moses. (Rom 5:14 ESV)

> We know that Christ, being raised from the dead, will never die again; death no longer has dominion over him. (Rom 6:9 ESV)

> The last enemy to be destroyed is death. (1 Cor 15:26 ESV)

Death is personified, but surely what 1 Cor 15:26 and Rev 20:14 mean is that death will no longer exist? It is not that Death as a person will suffer unending torment, but that it will cease to exist. When "death" enters the "second death" this means destruction, i.e., death ceases to exist, and "death shall be no more" (Rev 21:4).

Babylon, the Great Harlot, and the Beast

What about Babylon, the great harlot, and the great beast? Are they individuals or collections of individuals, and what will happen to them?

Whether the book of Revelation was completed soon after the death of Nero or much later in the reign of Domitian, many readers would have associated the beast with Nero and Rome. But surely the *Idealist* view must be right in taking the symbol to mean not only Nero/Rome but all earthly kingdoms which oppose the people of God on a "might is right" philosophy? Otherwise what relevance would it have to us?

Riding the beast is the harlot, but Revelation makes it clear that Babylon and the great harlot are the same entity:

---

16. Aune, *Revelation 6–16*, 401.

> And the woman that you saw is the great city that has dominion over the kings of the earth. (Rev 17:18 ESV)

Associated with the beast is the false prophet who deceives people about the beast.

The city and the harlot parallel the new Jerusalem and the bride of Christ. They represent greed, avarice, self-centeredness, and service of mammon. They are not individuals, nor even exclusively specific institutions, and they will be destroyed:

> Fallen, fallen is Babylon the great! . . . For all the nations have drunk of the wine of the passion of her fornication. (Rev 18:2–3 ESV)

> Her plagues will come in a single day, death and mourning and famine, and she will be burned up with fire; for mighty is the Lord God who has judged her. (Rev 18:8 ESV)

> And the kings of the earth, who committed sexual immorality and lived in luxury with her, will weep and wail over her when they see the smoke of her burning. They will stand far off, in fear of her torment, and say, "Alas! Alas! You great city, you mighty city, Babylon! For in a single hour your judgment has come." (Rev 18:9–10 ESV; also 18:17)

> The merchants of these wares, who gained wealth from her, will stand far off, in fear of her torment, weeping and mourning aloud. (Rev 18:15 ESV)

> So will Babylon the great city be thrown down with violence, and will be found no more. (Rev 18:21 ESV)

> Once more they cried out "Hallelujah! The smoke from her goes up for ever and ever." (Rev 19:3 ESV)

The city/harlot will be destroyed in a single day, and the smoke of her destruction will rise for ever and ever. The smoke is not indicating some continuing torture, but the memory and enduring effect of her destruction.

What of the beast and false prophet? These are obvious counterparts to the Lamb and Holy Spirit, but are they individuals? This seems highly unlikely. The imagery in Daniel has beasts/animals as symbols of kingdoms, symbols of ideologies. So then we read:

> And the beast was captured, and with it the false prophet who in its presence had done the signs by which he deceived those who had received the mark of the beast and those who worshiped its image. These two were thrown alive into the lake of fire that burns with sulfur. (Rev 19:20 ESV)

> And they marched up over the broad plain of the earth and surrounded the camp of the saints and the beloved city, but fire came down from heaven and consumed them, and the devil who had deceived them was thrown into the lake of fire and sulfur where the beast and the false prophet were, and they will be tormented day and night forever and ever. (Rev 20:9–10 ESV)

Most likely the beast and false prophet are no more individuals than the city and the harlot. Even Beale, who believes in unending torment, says:

> "The beast and the false prophet" are not literal but figurative for unbelieving institutions composed of people. Even "day and night" is not literal but figurative for the idea of the unceasing nature of the torment (see on 14:11). Strictly speaking, even the expression "they will be tormented for ever and ever" is figurative: . . . (it) literally can be rendered "unto the ages of the ages"; at the least the phrase figuratively connotes a very long time.[17]

How can an institution be tormented for a long time? Maybe it can go into a slow decline—but obviously not literally forever. H. B. Swete says that

> since two of the three subjects of the [torment] represent systems and not persons, it is safer to regard them

---

17. Beale, *Book of Revelation*, 1030.

as belonging to the scenery of the vision rather than to eschatological teaching.[18]

More recently Ian Paul, a theological conservative who is on the Anglican General Synod, writes:

> In interpreting the language of *torment . . . for ever and ever*, we need to consider at least three things. First, the dragon, beast and false prophet are metaphors for spiritual agents and systems opposed to God, rather than human agents. Second, the theme throughout these judgment chapters (from Rev 17 onwards) has been the principle of *lex talionis* and the justice of God's judgments, so the punishment is more severe for the agencies of deception than for those who were deceived. Third, the primary significance of the lake of fire and Sulphur, going right back to its origins in the Old Testament, is destruction rather than continual torture.[19]

Surely the beast represents a kind of "might is right" ideology (personified in many entities, with maybe a starting one in Nero's Rome), while the false prophet tells lies to draw people toward it. It is, therefore, hard to see Rev 20:10 as being about two individuals suffering unending torment, rather than the final destruction of the "might is right" ideology and the lies which accompany it.

What about Satan?

In volume 1 of *God's Strategy in Human History* we looked in detail at what we know of "the Satan" in the Bible. It does seem to refer to an individual who opposes God and corrupts mankind, but we really don't know much about his background. Was he created immortal or given a choice of immortality? The book of Job begins with a setting in which the "sons of God" "came and presented themselves" before *Yahweh*. John F. Hartley explains:

---

18. Swete, *Apocalypse of St John*, 270.

19. Paul, *Revelation*, 331, italics original.

On this occasion the Satan also came among them. Here
the Hebrew word *haśśāṭān* has the [definite] article so it
functions as a title rather than as a personal name.[20]

Here and in Zech 3:1 it is "the Satan," but the LXX or Septuagint version, translated from Hebrew to Greek by the Jews a
couple of centuries before Christ, translates it *diabolos*, and we
can clearly identify him with "Satan" or "the devil" in the gospels.
When Jesus was tempted by the devil, he addressed him as Satan.
Hartley explains that scholars differ as to whether *the Satan* was
one of the "sons of God," though traditionally he has been seen as
such (and Clines seems to agree). In Rev 12:9 the devil and Satan
are identified as the same, and apparently he has angels with him.
So the Satan seems to be an individual, but there is a lot we don't
know about him.

The book 1 Enoch (as above) states that the watchers (the
fallen angels) are immortal, and bear much more guilt than the
humans they have corrupted. So, does "to the ages of ages" (*tous
aiōnas tōn aiōnōn* in Rev 20:10) mean that Satan's suffering will be
literally unending? If the term is to be taken as indicative of duration rather than dimension or quality then maybe it does—though
the presence of the symbolic beast and false prophet might give us
some doubt.

Humans in the Lake of Fire

In Rev 20:9–10 we may note the contrast that fire from heaven
"consumed" the wicked deceived by Satan, in contrast to the fate
given for Satan himself.

Revelation 14:9–11 contains really the *only* passage in Scripture that could be taken to imply endless human suffering:

> And another angel, a third, followed them, saying with
> a loud voice, "If anyone worships the beast and its im-
> age and receives a mark on his forehead or on his hand,
> he also will drink the wine of God's wrath, poured full

20. Hartley, *Book of Job*, 71.

strength into the cup of his anger, and he will be tormented with fire and sulfur in the presence of the holy angels and in the presence of the Lamb. And the smoke of their torment goes up forever and ever, and they have no rest, day or night, these worshipers of the beast and its image, and whoever receives the mark of its name." (Rev 14:9–11 ESV)

Then Death and Hades were thrown into the lake of fire. This is the second death, the lake of fire. And if anyone's name was not found written in the book of life, he was thrown into the lake of fire. (Rev 20:14 ESV)

In general smoke rises as a memorial of destruction. When Abraham went out the morning after Sodom was destroyed he saw "dense smoke rising from the land, like smoke from a furnace" (Gen 19:28). This was signifying total destruction—nothing was left. Jude says:

Likewise, Sodom and Gomorrah and the surrounding cities, which, in the same manner as they, indulged in sexual immorality and pursued unnatural lust, serve as an example by undergoing a punishment of eternal fire. (Jude 7 NRSV)

The fire was eternal, but of course the cities were totally destroyed and ceased to exist. Second Peter 2:6 likewise notes that the "catastrophe" that overtook Sodom and Gomorrah was to be reduced to ashes, they were totally destroyed by judgmental fire and sulfur. The book of Wisdom says that when the fire came on the cities:

Evidence of their wickedness still remains: a continually smoking wasteland, plants bearing fruit that does not ripen, and a pillar of salt standing as a monument to an unbelieving soul. (Wis 10:7 NRSV)

Bauckham notes that in the first-century days of Josephus and Philo the smoking wastes were still pointed to;[21] but of course there was no idea of continuing suffering of those destroyed.

21. Bauckham, *Jude, 2 Peter*, 55, 251–52.

In Isaiah the prophecy of destruction is:

> For the LORD has a day of vengeance, a year of vindication by Zion's cause. And the streams of Edom shall be turned into pitch, and her soil into sulfur; her land shall become burning pitch. Night and day it shall not be quenched; its smoke shall go up for ever. From generation to generation it shall lie waste; no one shall pass through it for ever and ever. But the hawk and the hedgehog shall possess it; the owl and the raven shall live in it. (Isa 34:8–11 NRSV)

This is not speaking of unending suffering, but longtime smoke, commemorating total destruction. Ian Paul rightly comments on this verse:

> Though the phrase *smoke of their torment rises for ever and ever* (AT) has been interpreted as indicating a continual experience of torment . . . this is difficult to sustain in the light of the parallel at 19:3, where an identical phrase the "smoke from [the city, Babylon] rises for ever and ever" (AT). It is impossible to imagine the city being perpetually destroyed, the image must signify the eternal *effect* of its destruction rather than an eternal *process* of destruction.[22]

Does the language in 14:10 of "day and night" imply unending activity, i.e., unending suffering? This is a linguistic point, and G. K. Beale in his scholarly book states:

> But there is theological debate about the nature of final judgment. Does the portrayal mean that unbelievers are to be annihilated, so that their existence will be abolished forever? Or does this text refer to a destruction involving not absolute annihilation but the suffering of unbelievers for eternity? The OT context of Isa 34 could support the former view, since there the historical annihilation of Edom is portrayed. The image of continually ascending smoke in Isaiah 34 serves as a message of God's annihilating punishment for sin, the message of which never

---

22. Paul, *Revelation*, 250, italics original.

goes out of date (see Wis. 10:6–7; cf. Sodom in Ge 19:28). Likewise, to an escalated degree, in Jude 7 Sodom is set forth as an example of [others] undergoing the punishment of eternal fire. Accordingly, the lack of rest "night and day" also has its background in Isa 34:9, where, like the smoke, it refers to the enduring effects of the destruction of Edom. In particular "day and night" . . . in 14:11 can be taken as a qualitative genitive construction indicating not duration of time (like the accusative construction of the same phrase) but kind of time, that is, of ceaseless activity (e.g., Mark 5:5; Luke 18:7; Acts 9:24; 1 Thess 2:9; 3:10; 2 Thess 3:8; 1 Tim 5:5; 2 Tim 1:3; so also the LXX of Pss 21[22]:3[2]; . . .) The lack of rest will *continue uninterrupted*; as long as the period of suffering lasts, though there will be an end to the period. Therefore, the imagery of Rev 14:10–11 could indicate a great judgment that will be remembered forever, not one that leads to eternal suffering.[23]

Beale himself seems inclined to accept unending torment, and gives these reasons:

1. Because of the analogy with the fate of Satan in 19:20 and 20:10.

2. The word for "torment," he says, "is used nowhere in Revelation in the sense of annihilation of personal existence."

3. Reference to "eternal torment" for humans is found in apocryphal literature.

None of these seems convincing.

The first assumes that the effects of the lake of fire must be the same for Satan as for humans—a big assumption since humans are mortal. Caird assumes that the lake of fire for humans means "the annihilation of second death"[24]—which is what Rev 20:14 says.

Also, as noted, we do not know how and if Satan became immortal. The precursor imagery in 1 Enoch notes that the spirit we might identify as Satan is different from humans, and has much

23. Beale, *Book of Revelation*, 762, italics original.
24. Caird, *Revelation of St John the Divine*, 260.

greater guilt. And does it make sense? Are those who "worship the beast" to be identified with *all* who lack Judeo-Christian faith? So does Rev 20:14 really mean that this unending suffering without hope will befall a girl who grew up in a Muslim family, or a boy in a Hindu family who knew about Jesus only as a prophet or a god and who died of cancer at the age of five or six? Will she or he be suffering torment unendingly and without hope along with Satan? What kind of a God would this be? It would be a heavy doctrine to place solely on an interpretation of a single verse in such a highly metaphorical and complex book of visions. Another problem with the argument is that the implication for Death and Hades being thrown into the lake of fire is surely that they cease to exist—this is "the second death". Immediately after this the same fate is promised to anyone not in the Lamb's book of life.

On the second of Beale's three arguments, no one suggests that "torment" in itself *means* annihilation; certainly it means conscious suffering. But in, e.g., 2 Maccabees the brothers were "tormented" by the wicked king as part of the process of their final destruction (from his point of view) in death. The contention of those like the present author who believe in final destruction of the unrepentant is that any humans who suffer "torment" do so in the process by which they are finally destroyed/annihilated. Of course the term "torment" does not mean annihilation, but surely neither does the repeated term "destruction" mean unending torment?

On the third argument, apocryphal apocalyptic writings do speak of destruction. We already noted that the two most frequently cited to argue from unending torment from apocryphal writings (Judith and 4 Maccabees) are poor bases to determine what was the general NT apostolic belief. We should therefore surely want proper evidence in the NT itself that unending torment was the general Christian belief?

Stephen S. Smalley is influenced by Beale but has a different conclusion:

> The key theological issue raised by verse 11 is whether John means that those who reject Christ in favor of materialistic values will literally suffer divine judgment

forever, although it is the case that literal interpretations of the Apocalypse are always likely to be problematic. Some commentators certainly accept that the writer is speaking here not of the annihilation of unbelievers, but of their suffering throughout eternity. . . . Such a picture of unremitting punishment by God, however, calls into question both the justice and character of God and indeed his saving purposes for the world. . . .

An alternative way of understanding this passage of the Apocalypse, therefore, is to interpret the declarations that the unfaithful with be tormented "for ever" and that their suffering will be unremitting (continuing "day and night") in qualitative terms. The descriptions of the time-span involved in God's judgment, that is to say, do not indicate the duration of a temporal period, but the *kind* of time which is involved. Elsewhere in the biblical literature, for example, "day and night" indicates a period of ceaseless activity . . . which is intense while it lasts but will not last forever. In the same way, the angel is saying, the ongoing torment of the wicked will be uninterrupted while their suffering continues, but there will be a conclusion to that period.[25]

G. B. Caird states on Rev 14:9–11:

If we protest that we cannot accommodate our minds to the idea of eternal torment, the answer is that neither could John. He believed that, if at the end there should be any who remained impervious to the grace and love of God, they would be thrown with Death and Hades, into the lake of fire which is the second death, i.e., extinction and total oblivion.[26]

So Rev 14:9–11 speaks of the restlessness of those who worship the beast (which we see around us in effect today), and they ultimately await the anguish/torment when they are finally exposed to the fire of God (which I personally take to be his pure

---

25. Smalley, *Revelation to John*, 367–68, italics original.

26. Caird, *Language and Imagery of the Bible*, 186.

love). Their bodies and *psychēs* (souls) will be destroyed in this *Gehenna* as Jesus taught.

Some Conclusions on Revelation

1. The consistent teaching in plain theological sections of the NT is that the finally impenitent will be destroyed, i.e., will perish and cease to exist.

2. Revelation is a book containing prophetic apocalyptic visions, and it would be dangerous to draw from these doctrines not taught plainly elsewhere in the NT.

3. If the lake of fire is to be identified with what Jesus calls *Gehenna* then what God does in it to unrepentant humans is to destroy body and *psychē*.

4. The only verse (20:10) which could indicate actual unending suffering refers to the symbolic entities of the beast and false prophet, and also to Satan, and we do not know enough about his nature, immortality, etc., to be very dogmatic about what it means.

5

Some Conclusions

Conclusions on Hell and Destruction

The NT does not teach the Greek idea that humans are inherently immortal. Eternal life is a quality of life given now, and "incorruption" will be a gift when we rise again. If the unrighteous continue to exist this will be because God chooses for them to.

The Bible is plain that God does not want anyone to "perish" so he sent his Son to die for the sins of the world so that anyone who has faith will not perish but have eternal life. Plainly too the experience of the second death, i.e., of "perishing," is painful. But there is no indication that it involves suffering for unending time without hope or respite.

The NT (and OT) passages consistently seem to indicate that the final fate of the unrighteous is destruction, i.e., extinction. One or two ambiguous verses in the apocalyptic vision of Revelation could be read otherwise, but it is better to interpret them in line with the clearer statements in plain-speaking NT theology.

The Nature of God and Judgment

Destruction and Justice

Most of the New Testament authors give explicit teaching that God will destroy (meaning utterly consume or annihilate) the finally unrepentant. Those who believe that hell involves unending suffering without hope cannot point to any plain, straightforward theological statement which states this. Rather they have to rely on highly questionable interpretations of complex allusions in parables or apocalyptic images. All this leaves little room for doubt about the nature of hell and the final fate of destruction for those who remain unrepentant.

God as judge features high in the OT, but Powys says:

> The early traditions do not indicate a strong association between punishment and judgment in the functions of Israel's judges.[1]

> Vengeance . . . is not a major theme anywhere in the OT, and in no case is there any suggestion that any will experience God's vengeance after death.[2]

> Punishment in the Old Testament is rarely if ever an end in itself.[3]

Throughout the OT, punishment was either corrective or to "put away the evil from among you" by destroying its agents. So we need to be very careful if we import to God's justice ideas of indefinite suffering.

If someone rejects God, then does God still love them? God commends his love for us in that while we were still sinners Jesus died for us. Even sinners, Jesus says, love their friends:

> But love your enemies, and do good, and lend, expecting nothing in return, and your reward will be great, and you will be sons of the Most High, for he is kind to the

1. Powys, "Hell," 73.
2. Powys, "Hell," 82.
3. Powys, "Hell," 176.

ungrateful and the evil. Be merciful, even as your Father is merciful. (Luke 6:35–36 ESV)

As sons of God we will love *all* our enemies—as he does. It was "the world" that he loved and for which he sent his Son, and he would like everyone to repent and come to a knowledge of the truth.

So one might ask those who believe in hell as torment for unlimited time, could God not make these sufferers cease to exist if he so chose? If he cannot then he must be weak. If he can and will not then he cannot love them. Quite bizarre is the claim of Habermas and Moreland:

> It is clearly more immoral to extinguish humans with intrinsic value than to allow them to continue living in a state with a low quality of life.[4]

Having a "low quality of life"?! Suffering the supposed pangs of unending extreme torment with *no hope* of ever experiencing relief? Would Habermas and Moreland *really* rather that someone they loved would simply cease to exist, or would live in nonstop torment, forever, *without hope*, through endless time? What a strange idea of what is immoral. Were there hope of eventual redemption this might make sense, but not otherwise. If you are a Christian, then think of someone you loved dearly in this life, but who never became a Christian. Would you feel happy to be in a new heaven and earth where there was "nothing to hurt or destroy" but you were in knowledge that this loved one was suffering, without hope, for unlimited time? To suggest that we will all be so busy having a good time that it will not bother us, or that somehow we will feel it "serves them right," seems to sit ill with the kind of righteous, loving people Jesus wanted us to become.

None of this is to "judge God" but to judge the strange ideas of some theologians about God; ideas which are not in the Bible.

---

4. Habermas and Moreland, *Beyond Death*, 173.

Some Speculative Ideas on Love and Fire

How should we hold together the ideas of the love and wrath of God? Scripture does not do this explicitly for us, but maybe there are some hints about it, so here are some speculative suggestions.

A core biblical teaching is the *Shema*: "Hear, O Israel: the Lord our God, the Lord is one" (Deut 6:4). Surely God is not a split personality. We should not *contrast* God's love with his wrath or justice. God is *love* (1 John 4:8,16), God is *light* (1 John 1:5), and God is a *consuming fire* (Heb 12:29, quoting Deut 4:23–25). In a sense these are all the same, and all are eternal because they are a part of his nature. God's love/light exposes evil for what it is and consumes it. Those who reject and resist it will ultimately be consumed by it in judgment—and this experience will be painful. How people experience God depends on their reaction to and relationship with him. Throughout the prophecies and Psalms it is clear that, depending on whether or not people have a faith relationship with him, their experience may be of love or wrath. But God is the same.

In Exod 24:17 the sight of the glory of the LORD was like a consuming fire on the top of the mountain in the eyes of the children of Israel. In Exod 33:5 God could not (as Moses asked) go down among the Israelites, for it would consume them. Later in Exod 33, even Moses could not see the pure face of God, but when he saw just part of this then his own face shone with God's glory so that he had to veil it in meeting the other Jews. So the sight of God which was refining and elevating for Moses would have destroyed the ungodly.

An interesting earthly parallel is when the three Jews in Daniel 3 were thrown into a fiery furnace. The fire freed them and did not even singe them, but it killed the guards.

The same *fire* of the *love* of God will engulf believers on the Day. The righteous saints are building the temple of God, the church. On the Day, each person's work in this regard will be tried by the fire. Wood, hay, and stubble will be consumed, and only precious materials survive (1 Cor 3:12–17). Anything we as

Christians build into the church will be tested by this *fire* of God's love.

Some have asked how the fire of *Gehenna* can be eternal if the wicked have all been consumed. Maybe the "fire" of hell is eternal because the pure love of God is like an eternal otherworldly fire.

Having said this, there will remain mysteries concerning time and eternity. One final idea can be brought into this from science. A person falling into a black hole appears to a distant observer to slow down, and hover just above it. But from the point of view of the person, he or she does fall in, and get crushed by the singularity at the center of the black hole in a finite time. If this works in physics then it is entirely possible that in the process of spiritual judgment the person being judged experiences a process which takes a finite time, whereas to other observers it would appear timeless? Would this explain the smoke of their torment going up forever?

Universalism and Second Chances

Finally, a word about the portal or universalist views. Universalists (as, e.g., in MacDonald),[5] like those of us who believe hell implies destruction, all believe in a God of Love. The difference is that the latter believe that Love will not override freewill, and so people who ultimately reject the Love of God will be destroyed by it. Universalists believe that ultimately all human freewill will be overcome by God's sovereign Love and everyone will be redeemed. However, the language of Scripture seems to indicate that *destruction* will be the final reality for those who continue to reject God's free offer of forgiveness and salvation and this seems incompatible with universalism.

Could there be any "second chance" after death to repent, or even a continuing chance over extended time? This is not referring here to those who throughout life sought "glory and honor, and immortality" (Romans chapter 2) without hearing of Jesus,

---

5. MacDonald, *Evangelical Universalist.*

and will be given eternal life through him at the judgment. It is about those who did know about and reject in this life the "light that enlightens everyone who comes into the world." Well, we may remember that when God sent Jonah to Nineveh there was no mention of any chance to repent—but God changed his mind! The Living Bible pithily puts it:

> And when God saw that they had put a stop to their evil ways, he abandoned his plan to destroy them and didn't carry it through. (Jonah 3:10 TLB; see also Exod 32:14 and 1 Chr 21:15)

Jonah was angry and complained to God that he knew God was "a gracious and merciful God, slow to anger, and abundant in lovingkindness, One who relents from doing harm." God is not fickle and has never failed to fulfill a promise to those who continue in steadfast love to him, but Jonah knew that God could change his mind if he saw an opportunity to show mercy. Jonah was not mandated to declare the possibility of repentance and forgiveness, but he knew it was always possible. We are not mandated to declare that there is any second or third chance after death, but it would be a bold theologian who told God that he could not change his mind if there were an opportunity to show mercy. Not even Jonah did that, but he was angry when it happened.

Preaching the Gospel

Those of us who accept the biblical teaching that the wicked will be destroyed may be termed "conditionalists" or "annihilationists" but acceptance of the fact that the Bible teaches the final end of the unrepentant will be destruction is not an "ism." It seeks only to be true to Scripture and the God and Father of our Lord Jesus the Messiah. So we will continue to declare what God has mandated us to declare:

> See, the day is coming, burning like an oven, when all the arrogant and all evildoers will be stubble; the day that comes shall burn them up, says the LORD of hosts, so

that it will leave them neither root nor branch. But to you who fear my name, the Sun of Righteousness shall arise with healing in His wings. (Mal 4:1 NRSV)

As Christians we are building the church, including ourselves as part of it, but Paul makes clear that if we do not build based on love then our works are like wood, hay, and stubble. The *fire* on the day of judgment will test our lives:

> Now if anyone builds on the foundation with gold, silver, precious stones, wood, hay, straw—the work of each builder will become visible, for the Day will disclose it, because it will be revealed with fire, and the fire will test what sort of work each has done. If what has been built on the foundation survives, the builder will receive a reward. If the work is burned, the builder will suffer loss; the builder will be saved, but only as through fire. (1 Cor 3:12–14 NRSV)

Although we will face judgment, we do not fear because we are already based in the love of God.

> Love has been perfected among us in this: that we may have boldness on the day of judgment, because as he is, so are we in this world. There is no fear in love, but perfect love casts out fear; for fear has to do with punishment, and whoever fears has not reached perfection in love. (1 John 4:1–18 NRSV)

All this last is clear. Also, we have forgiveness and relationship with God through our faith in Jesus. Because Jesus became sin for us, he drank the cup of God's wrath—he experienced the pain of the exposure to that fire of Love in a sinful state beyond our dreams. He accepted the cup, even though he longed not to have to do this, but it was (it seems) the only way. Because of who he was, the cup of wrath/fire did not destroy him, and he rose again, and whoever believes in him will not be destroyed, but have eternal life.

6

Early Historical Teachings

All the early Christian writers believed that there would be a judgment, and that the unrepentant would suffer hellfire. A key question was whether human souls were immortal. If not, then the hellfire judgment could be a process leading to total destruction. If souls were immortal, then this option was not possible (though no one seems to have suggested that God *could not* simply annihilate them).

Some earliest Christian writings, like the *Epistle of Barnabas, Ignatius to the Ephesians, 2 Clement,* and *Martyrdom of Polycarp,* simply do not indicate whether they believe suffering in hellfire to be unending or leading to final destruction. Second Clement 6:7 does not say what the eternal punishment is, and 17:5–7 refers to the torments "in the Day of judgment" but does not indicate they will be interminable. The Shepherd of Hermas Parable 6 in 62:4 says unrepentance leads to "death," which it describes as "eternal destruction (*apōleian aiōnion*)"; it has no indication anywhere of unending suffering.

Powys,[1] Fudge,[2] and E. Earle Ellis[3] show how mainstream Christian teachers like Justin Martyr, Irenaeus, Arnobius, Theophilus, and Athanasius all teach against the immortality of the human soul. Those who believed the human soul to be immortal, either held that suffering was unending (e.g., Anaxagoras, Tatian, and Tertullian) or that the immortal humans suffering in hell could eventually repent and be saved (e.g., Origen speculatively and Gregory of Nyssa more definitely).

Here we will look at two of the earliest Christian leaders, both central in the defence of New Testament faith against critics and heresy, both of whom spoke the language of the New Testament. As already indicated, Christian doctrine should be taken from Scripture, not from any commentators, but if the biblical understanding of hellfire espoused in this book is correct then it would not be a surprise to find the most learned of earliest Christian thinkers, who were closest in time and language to the apostles, taking a similar line. The fire itself is everlasting, but the judgment suffering it causes is not.

Justin Martyr (ca. 100–165)

Justin was a philosopher who became a Christian and was martyred for his faith. His first language was Greek, and he studied Hebrew, and debated with a Jewish rabbi. In our *God's Strategy in Human History* we show how closely Justin follows New Testament theology.[4] On the present issue, he is quite clear. In his *First Apology* 52, he states that all will be raised to judgment, but implies that human souls are not immortal, and says only those worthy will be given immortality; the wicked will go into the eternal fire and worms (as Jesus said). He does not hold that human souls are

---

1. Powys, *"Hell,"* chapter 1.

2. Fudge, *Fire That Consumes*, chapter 24.

3. Ellis in Brower and Elliott, *Eschatology in Bible and Theology*, chapter 9.

4. Forster and Marston, *God's Strategy in Human History*, 2nd ed, 292–96, or Forster and Marston, *God's Strategy in Human History*, 3rd ed, 2:229–33.

immortal, but rather that continuation is a gift of God.[5] In his *Second Apology* 7, he states:

> Wherefore God delays causing the confusion and destruction of the whole world, *by which the wicked angels and demons and men shall cease to exist*, because of the seed of the Christians, who know that they are the cause of preservation in nature . . . since God in the beginning made the race of angels and men with free-will, they will justly suffer in eternal fire the punishment of whatever sins they have committed.[6]

Justin Martyr believes that eternal fire and worms of Gehenna will cause people to suffer punishment, but is explicit that in the end they will *cease to exist*. This is what Scripture teaches. "Destruction" means that finally they cease to exist.

Irenaeus of Gaul (ca. 130–200)

Irenaeus was the great defender of the mainstream biblical faith against the gnostic heresies. In his great work *Against Heresies* Irenaeus seems clear that immortality is not inherent in humankind but is a gift of God to the believers.

So, we find, e.g., in *Against Heresies* 1:10:

> He [Jesus] should execute just judgment toward all; that he may send "spiritual wickedness," and the angels who transgressed and became apostates, together with the ungodly and unrighteous and wicked and profane amongst men into everlasting fire; but *may in exercise of his grace confer immortality on the righteous*.[7]

In 2:29 again he speaks of "those who enter into immortality." In 2:34 we read:

> 2. But if any persons at this point maintain that those souls, which only began a little while ago to exist, cannot

5. Roberts and Donaldson, *Ante-Nicene Fathers*, 1:180, italics added.
6. Roberts and Donaldson, *Ante-Nicene Fathers*, 1:190, italics added.
7. Roberts and Donaldson, *Ante-Nicene Fathers*, 1:350–51, italics added..

endure for any length of time; but that they must, on the one hand, either be unborn, in order that they may be immortal, or if they have had a beginning in the way of generation, that they should die with the body itself—let them learn that God alone, who is Lord of all, is without beginning and without end, being truly and for ever the same, and always remaining the same unchangeable Being. But all things which proceed from Him, whatsoever have been made, and are made, do indeed receive their own beginning of generation, and on this account are inferior to Him who formed them, inasmuch as they are not unbegotten. Nevertheless they endure, and extend their existence into a long series of ages in accordance with the will of God their Creator; so that He grants them that they should be thus formed at the beginning, and that they should so exist afterwards.

3. For as the heaven which is above us, the firmament, the sun, the moon, the rest of the stars, and all their grandeur, although they had no previous existence, were called into being, and continue throughout a long course of time according to the will of God, so also any one who thinks thus respecting souls and spirits, and, in fact, respecting all created things, will not by any means go far astray, inasmuch as all *things that have been made had a beginning when they were formed, but endure as long as God wills that they should have an existence and continuance.* The prophetic Spirit bears testimony to these opinions, when He declares, For He spoke, and they were made; He commanded, and they were created: He has established them for ever, yea, forever and ever. And again, He thus speaks respecting the salvation of man: He asked life of You, and You gave him length of days for ever and ever; indicating that it is the Father of all who imparts continuance for ever and ever on those who are saved. *For life does not arise from us, nor from our own nature; but it is bestowed according to the grace of God.* And therefore he who shall preserve the life bestowed upon him, and give thanks to Him who imparted it, shall receive also length of days for ever and ever. But *he who shall reject it, and prove himself ungrateful to his Maker,*

inasmuch as he has been created, and has not recognised Him who bestowed [the gift upon him], deprives himself of [the privilege of] continuance for ever and ever. And, for this reason, the Lord declared to those who showed themselves ungrateful toward Him: If ye have not been faithful in that which is little, who will give you that which is great? indicating that those who, in this brief temporal life, have shown themselves ungrateful to Him who bestowed it, shall justly not receive from Him length of days for ever and ever.[8]

This is quite clear. Unending existence is a gift of God given to those who worship and turn to God, and those who do not repent deprive themselves of it. The unrighteous deprive themselves of this gift and shall not receive "length of days for ever and ever." This is not just length of *happy* days for ever and ever, but the length of *any* days for ever and ever.

In Book 5:1.1 Irenaeus says that Christ will "bestow on us immortality" at his *parousia*. Immortality is not inherent. In 5:3.2 again it is at the resurrection we are given immortality. In 5:11.1 the fate of those who live after the flesh is "destruction." It is in light of this that we can read the later passage in 5:27.2 which is sometimes cited by those who claim that Irenaeus believed in unending torment for unbelievers:

> 2. And to as many as continue in their love towards God, does He grant communion with Him. But communion with God is life and light, and the enjoyment of all the benefits which He has in store. *But on as many as, according to their own choice, depart from God, He inflicts that separation from Himself which they have chosen of their own accord. But separation from God is death, and separation from light is darkness; and separation from God consists in the loss of all the benefits which He has in store.* Those, therefore, who cast away by apostasy these aforementioned things, being in fact destitute of all good, do experience every kind of punishment. God, however, does not punish them immediately of Himself, but that

---

8. Roberts and Donaldson, *Ante-Nicene Fathers*, 1:411–12, italics added.

punishment falls upon them because they are destitute of all that is good. *Now, good things are eternal and without end with God, and therefore the loss of these is also eternal and never-ending.* It is in this matter just as occurs in the case of a flood of light: those who have blinded themselves, or have been blinded by others, are for ever deprived of the enjoyment of light. It is not, [however], that the light has inflicted upon them the penalty of blindness, but it is that the blindness itself has brought calamity upon them: and therefore the Lord declared, "He that believe in Me is not condemned, that is, is not separated from God, for he is united to God through faith. On the other hand, He says, He that believeth not is condemned already, because he has not believed in the name of the only-begotten Son of God; that is, he separated himself from God of his own accord. For this is the condemnation, that light has come into this world, and men have loved darkness rather than light. For everyone who doesth evil hateth the light, and cometh not to the light, lest his deeds should be reproved. But he that doe truth cometh to the light, that his deeds may be made manifest, that he has wrought them in God.[9]

He says separation from God is death, and separation from light is darkness; and separation from God consists in the loss of all the benefits which he has in store. Part of these gifts (as Irenaeus has earlier noted) is "continuance for ever and ever" and anyone who rejects God "deprives himself of [the privilege of] continuance for ever and ever." The punishment is eternal because the effect of losing this gift of continuance is permanent. This is clearly meant in saying: "Good things are eternal and without end with God, and therefore the loss of these is also eternal and never-ending." God's gift is immortality and eternal life, and to miss out on these is an eternal punishment. This reflects the language In Matt 25:46. To forfeit the possibility of eternal life is an *eternal punishment*—a permanent deprivation.

9. Roberts and Donaldson, *Ante-Nicene Fathers*, 1:556, italics added.

Powys also gives a detailed analysis of Irenaeus, showing that he believes neither in the immortality of the soul nor in unending suffering in hellfire.

Conclusions

The immortality of the human soul, and consequent unending suffering of the unrepentant for unending time without hope, later became entrenched in theological tradition. But two of the earliest Christian leaders, most learned and closest in language to the New Testament, did clearly accept the biblical teaching that the ultimate fate of the wicked after judgment is destruction.

Bibliography

Abbott-Smith, G. *Manual Greek Lexicon*. 3rd ed. Edinburgh: Clark, 1991.

Atkinson, Basil. *Life and Immortality*. Taunton, UK: Phoenix Press, 1969.

Aune, David E. *Word Biblical Commentary Revelation 1–5, 6–16, 17–22*. Dallas: Word, 1998.

Bauckham, Richard. *The Fate of the Dead*. Supplements to Novum Testamentum 93. Leiden: Brill, 1998.

———. "The Rich Man and Lazarus: The Parable and the Parallels." *New Testament Studies* 37 (1991) 225–46.

———. *The Theology of the Book of Revelation*. Cambridge: Cambridge University Press, 2002.

———. *Word Biblical Commentary Jude, 2 Peter*. Dallas: Word, 1983.

Beale, G. K. *The Book of Revelation*. New International Greek Testament Commentary. Grand Rapids: Eerdmans, 1998.

Bell, Rob. *Love Wins*. San Francisco: HarperOne, 2011.

Blomberg, Craig L. *Interpreting the Parables*. Downers Grove, IL: InterVarsity, 2011.

Brower, Kent E., and Mark W. Elliott. *Eschatology in Bible and Theology*. Downers Grove, IL: InterVarsity, 1997.

Brown, Colin, ed. *The New International Dictionary of New Testament Theology*. Rev. ed. 4 vols. Carlisle: Paternoster, 1992.

Caird, G. B. *The Language and Imagery of the Bible*. London: Bloomsbury, 1980.

———. *The Revelation of St John the Divine*. London: Black, 1966.

Charles R. H. *The Book of Enoch*. 1917. Reprint, New York: Dover, 2007.

Cornthwaite, Christopher J. "Torah in the Diaspora: A Comparative Study of Philo and 4 Maccabees." MA thesis, University of Western Ontario, 2013. https://ir.lib.uwo.ca/cgi/viewcontent.cgi?article=2584&context=etd.

DeSilver, David A. *Fourth Maccabees and the Promotion of the Jewish Philosophy*. Eugene, OR: Cascade, 2020.

Dudley-Smith, Timothy. *John Stott: A Global Ministry* Carlisle: InterVarsity, 2001.

Elledge, C. D. *Resurrection of the Dead in Early Judaism*. Oxford: Oxford University Press, 2017.

Fee, Gordon D., and Douglas Stewart. *How to Read the Bible for All Its Worth.* 4th ed. Grand Rapids: Zondervan, 2014.

Forster, Roger, and Paul Marston. *God's Strategy in Human History.* 2nd ed. Eugene, OR: Wipf & Stock, 2000.

———. *God's Strategy in Human History.* 2 vols. 3rd ed. London: Push, 2013.

France, R. T. *The Gospel of Mark.* New International Commentary on the New Testament. Grand Rapids: Eerdmans, 2002.

———. *The Gospel of Matthew.* New International Commentary on the New Testament. Grand Rapids: Eerdmans, 2007.

Fudge, Edward William. *The Fire That Consumes: A Biblical and Historical Study of the Doctrine of Final Punishment.* 3rd ed. Eugene, OR: Cascade, 2011.

Habermas, Gary, and J. P. Moreland. *Beyond Death.* Eugene, OR: Wipf & Stock, 2004.

Hartley, John F. *The Book of Job.* Word Bible Commentary. Dallas: Word, 1988.

Hatch, Edwin, and Henry A. Redpath. *A Concordance to the Septuagint.* 1897. Reprint, Oxford: Clarendon, 1954.

Hillborn, David. *The Nature of Hell: A Report by the Evangelical Alliance Commission on Unity and Truth among Evangelicals, ACUTE.* Carlisle: Paternoster, 2000.

Hooker, Morna A. D. *The Gospel according to Mark.* London: Black, 1991.

Kittel, Gerhard. *Theological Dictionary of the New Testament.* Grand Rapids: Eerdmans, 1966.

Klein, William W., et al. *Introduction to Biblical Interpretation.* 3rd ed. Grand Rapids: Zondervan Academic, 2017.

Longenecker, Richard N., ed. *Life in the Face of Death.* Grand Rapids: Eerdmans, 1998.

MacDonald, Gregory. *The Evangelical Universalist.* London: SPCK, 2014.

Marshall, Howard I. *The Gospel of Luke.* New International Greek Text Commentary. Exeter, UK: Paternoster, 1978.

Mounce, Robert H. *The Book of Revelation.* New International Commentary on the New Testament. Grand Rapids: Eerdmans, 1998.

Nickelsburg, George W. *A Commentary on the Book of 1 Enoch, Chapters 1–36, 81–108.* Minneapolis: Fortress, 2001.

———. *1 Enoch: A New Translation.* Minneapolis: Fortress, 2005.

Nolland, John. *The Gospel of Matthew: A Commentary on the Greek Text.* New International Greek Testament Commentary. Grand Rapids: Eerdmans, 2005.

———. *Luke 9:21–18:34.* Word Biblical Commentary. Dallas: Word, 1993.

Osborne, Grant R. *Revelation.* Baker Exegetical Commentary on the New Testament. Ada, MI: Baker Academic, 2002.

Papaioannou, Kim. *The Geography of Hell in the Teaching of Jesus: Gehenna, Hades, the Abyss, the Outer Darkness Where There Is Weeping and Gnashing of Teeth.* Eugene, OR: Pickwick, 2013.

Paul, Ian. *Revelation.* London: InterVarsity, 2018.

Penner, Ken. "Philo's Eschatology Personal and Cosmic." *Journal for the Study of Judaism* 50 (2019) 383–402.

Powys, David. *"Hell": A Hard Look at a Hard Question*. Carlisle, UK: Paternoster, 1997.

Roberts, Alexander, and James Donaldson, eds. *The Ante-Nicene Fathers*. 10 vols. Grand Rapids: Eerdmans, 1987.

Robertson, A. T. *A Grammar of the Greek New Testament in the Light of Historical Research*. Nashville: Broadman, 1934.

Smalley, Stephen S. *The Revelation to John: A Commentary on the Greek Text of the Apocalypse*. Downers Grove, IL: InterVarsity, 2005.

Swete, H. B. *The Apocalypse of St John*. London: Macmillan, 1909.

Thayer, Joseph Henry. *Greek English Lexicon of the New Testament*. New York: American Book Company, 1889.

VanGemeren, Willem A., ed. *New International Dictionary of Old Testament Theology and Exegesis*. 5 vols. Carlisle, UK: Paternoster, 1996.

Vermes, Geza. *The Complete Dead Sea Scrolls in English*. 7th ed. London: Penguin, 2004. Kindle edition.

Wenham, David. *The Parables of Jesus*. London: Hodder & Stoughton, 1989.

Wenham, John. *Facing Hell*. Carlisle, UK: Paternoster, 1998.

Witherington, Ben, III. *Revelation*. Cambridge: Cambridge University Press, 2003.

Wright, N. T. *The Resurrection of the Son of God*. Minneapolis: Fortress, 2003.

———. *Surprised by Hope*. London: SPCK, 2011.

Subject Index

Subject Index

eternal punishment, 1, 4, 33–36,
    40, 43, 45–47, 58, 60, 87, 92
eternal torment, 23, 50, 53, 58,
    76, 78
eternity, 30, 75, 78, 84
evangelical, 3, 5, 44–45, 64
evangelicals, 3, 6
exegesis, 6–7, 30, 67
extinction, 23, 29, 50, 60, 62, 78, 80

fallen angels, 15, 49–50, 62, 73
false prophet, 70–73, 79
final judgment, 11, 15, 22, 29, 45,
    58, 60–61, 63, 75
fire and worms, 48, 89
Futuristic, 67

Gē Hinnōm, 36–37, 51
Gehenna, 5, 26, 36–39, 47, 51, 55,
    79, 84, 89
genre, 7, 65–67
gnashing of teeth, 61, 64

Hades, 8–11, 13–16, 18–23, 36, 52,
    55, 57–58, 68–69, 74, 77–78
harlot, 69, 70–71
hell, 1–5, 29, 35–39, 45, 47, 53, 55,
    58, 80, 82, 84, 88
Hellenistic, 9, 52, 55
Hellenization, 21
Hellfire, 60, 87, 93
Heōs aiōnos, 48
hermeneutics, 6
Historicist, 67

Idealist, 67–69
immortal, 8–9, 11, 25, 46, 49–50,
    53–54, 72–73, 76, 80, 87–90
immortality, 45, 52–53, 56, 72, 79,
    84, 88–89, 91–93
incorruption, 9, 80
Irenaeus, 3, 46, 88–89, 91–93

Jonah, 85
Josephus, 9, 53–55, 74

judgment, 1– 2, 4, 11, 13–18,
    21–26, 28–29, 31–34, 36–39,
    41–43, 45–46, 48–49, 51–52,
    56–63, 66, 70, 72, 75–78, 81,
    83–89, 93
Judith, 47–48, 77
Justin Martyr, 3, 88–89

kolasin, 40–43, 45–46
kolazo, 40–42
krima, 33, 58

lake of fire, 22, 36, 62, 65, 68–69,
    71–74, 76–79
last judgment, 2, 15, 17–18, 49
Law and the Prophets, 18–19
Lazarus, 15–16, 18–20, 23, 60
lost, 2, 21, 23, 27–28
lost coin, 28
lost sheep, 27–28

Messiah, 18, 20, 25, 29, 61, 85

Nero, 68–69, 72

olethron, 34
Origen, 3, 54, 88
Orphic, 11–12, 16, 19
outer darkness, 60, 62–63

parable, 7, 12, 15–20, 22–23, 27,
    60–65, 87
parables, 20, 25, 28, 44, 60–61,
    63–65, 81
paradise, 13, 15, 20–21
parousia, 21, 43, 60, 64, 91
perish, 23, 25–29, 48–49, 59,
    79–80
perished, 29
perishing, 80
Pharisees, 9, 14, 18, 25, 53–54
Philo, 9, 53, 74
Plato, 9, 11–12, 16, 19, 46, 54
Preterist, 67
prodigal son, 28
Psalms of Solomon, 13, 52

Milton Keynes UK
Ingram Content Group UK Ltd.
UKHW022139070124
435463UK00003B/12

9 781666 784787